MW00939871

THE
STORY
TELLING
HEART

Nick Ovalle

ISBN: 1546518142
ISBN-13: 978-1546518143

DEDICATION

Dedicated to Brayden, Emerson & Arri. May the story you tell make a difference for future generations.

CONTENTS

ACKNOWLEDGMENTS

This book is possible because of the brave men and women who decided to pursue a field of study that looked at psychology, story, and marketing in a whole new light. It's those individuals' work that I have consumed and remixed to make this book.

LIFE HAS SECRETS.

COUNTERINTUITIVE SECRETS THAT CAN SPUR GREATNESS.

I have tried to collect as many secrets as I know and share them with the world.

Do you want to know the greatest secret I have ever encountered?

YOU ARE VALUABLE.

Many times we don't see our own value. In this ADHD world of on demand entertainment and cerebral experiences we often forget to breathe, let alone take time to think about our value. It pains me to think that some people spend so much time enthralled in distractions that they forget to take inventory of self. It's a scary thought to live and die and never know who you are / were.

HERE IS ANOTHER SECRET. IT'S NOT ENOUGH JUST TO KNOW THE SECRET. YOU

MUST ACT ON IT.

Not many people have the courage to tell you this, but I am not afraid of the backlash. You need to focus on yourself until "you can get you."

Esoteric right? Did that make your brain hurt?

The first time an author made my brain hurt was when Seth Godin talked about tribes. 'Niche down' was a principle Seth was trying to convey, but I believed mass adoption was the only way to success. After looking at the math, I saw Seth was right. It was an "aha!" moment when I realized I didn't know what I thought I knew.

You are valuable and you might not know it. You are valuable and you might not be focusing on yourself. I'm not talking about becoming a narcissist or elitist. I am talking about you changing the narrative in your mind that says you're not worth it. Your actions are the screenplay of your internal narrative. Bad writing, bad story, bad popcorn. We all hate a bad story but sometimes we don't know the secrets of storytelling that can change our own personal narrative.

This book is about those secrets. Counterintuitive as (insert your favorite explicative here) but they work.

The idea of "you being able to be you" is difficult.

WE CONSTANTLY LOOK TO OTHER PEOPLE FOR VALIDATION, FOR A ROAD MAP FOR LIFE, FOR SUCCESS, AND FOR FULFILLMENT. EVERY TIME I HAVE JOURNEYED DOWN THIS ROAD I HAVE BEEN SEVERELY DISSATISFIED. THE BEST WAY I CAN DESCRIBE "YOU GETTING YOU" IS TO "IMITATE YOURSELF."

The question that fuels this narrative change (Yes, questions are the fuel that will ultimately change your story) is, "What matters most?"

This places responsibility on your shoulders to make your dreams come true. Not very many people will take responsibility for your dreams.

SO WHAT WOULD YOU DO? IF YOU WERE IN CHARGE? IF YOU HAD TO CALL THE SHOTS? HOW DOES YOUR STORY GO? IN THE STORYTELLING HEART I HOPE TO GIVE YOU TOOLS TO HELP SHIFT YOUR PARADIGM.

I CAN'T WRITE THE ROAD MAP FOR YOU.

I CAN'T GIVE YOU A STEP BY STEP PROCESS TO CHANGE. WE ARE ALL SO VERY DIFFERENT AND UNIQUE. I FEEL THAT OFFERING A ONE SIZE FITS ALL APPROACH TO TELLING A BETTER STORY DOESN'T WORK.

EVER.

EVER. EVER. EVER.

WHY ROAD MAPS FAIL!

Road maps are other people's guides, other people's set of rules on how, when and why to live your life. Road maps fail because they are one dimensional and you live in more than one dimension. We struggle with road maps because they don't speak to why? They don't inspire. They don't speak to intention. They rarely speak to time. They don't speak to our fear or doubt. If someone is selling you a road map, chances are it won't work, or worse yet, it will work and you will find yourself in a place where you don't want to be.

1. Road Maps fail because nobody can tell you **WHO** you are.

2. Road Maps fail because nobody can tell you where **YOUR HAPPINESS** is.

3. Road Maps fail because there are no paved roads where you are headed.

4. Discovery is at the **HEART OF INNOVATION**. Maps kill discovery.

5. Maps are chic. Everyone is selling a good looking map.

6. Maps are two-dimensional. Your thought life, your story, is a **UNIVERSE**.

7. Road Maps fail because **THE JOURNEY IS ALWAYS INWARD**.

8. Learn to **NAVIGATE** and TEACH OTHERS TO NAVIGATE.

9. Don't give someone your personal road map. Help them develop their own.

10. Formulas are not road maps. Don't confuse the two.

Step by step processes only work for a few people. Lack of resource, education, time, or choice are all factors that will destroy a step by step process. ***Story is meant to be imitated and molded to fit our narrative.***

What I am proposing is that you become the hero of your own story. Taking responsibility for your story. Change the things you can and don't worry about the things you can't. It's with the utmost humility I thank you for letting me guide you to developing your story telling heart.

CHAPTER ONE:
EXPERIMENTS THAT INSPIRE

PLEASE FILL OUT THE FOLLOWING
INFORMATION:

NAME _____

AGE_____

FIRST CHILDHOOD
MEMORY_____

_____

MY HAPPIEST MOMENT_____

_____

MY DARKEST SECRET_____

_____

MY FAVORITE FOOD_____

_____

BEFORE I DIE I WANT TO_____

_____

These are all facts on a page. Facts on a page are not story. Well, not yet. Story engages us with rich meaning, with deep character development. Within story, tragedy can turn to triumph, the peasant can become the sultan, the sacrifice of two young lovers can end a civil war. The power of storytelling is taking facts and giving them rich context (surroundings) and rich subtext (meaning). These are two things that storytellers spend plenty of time crafting. The perfect surroundings and the perfect meaning to their characters.

STORY ENGAGES US WITH RICH MEANING, WITH DEEP CHARACTER DEVELOPMENT.

The ancient Hebrew people used to tell a story about **the book of life.** Moses and King David mention a book that has names in it. The original meaning of **the book of life** was to symbolize your life ending, that "God" was authoring your days before you lived them.

BEAUTIFUL POETRY.

If your appointed time to die came, your name would be removed from **the book of life** (Exodus 31:32-33, Psalms 69:27-28). The meaning transformed over the centuries to mean a list of names to get into heaven. Regardless of the origin, the story of the book of life continued and still continues to this day.

Why?!

 The ancients knew the power of storytelling was engrained in humanity, they believed "God" authored their story. You see many times in the works of the Christian Bible, Jesus being referred to as a storyteller, magician and author.

THE ANCIENTS KNEW THE POWER OF STORYTELLING WAS ENGRAINED IN HUMANITY. THEY BELIEVED 'GOD' AUTHORED THEIR STORY.

The power and craft of story was so vitally important to ancient civilization because it communicates meaning and belief. It teaches societal rules and inspires others to live to their full potential.

IF YOUR APPROACH TO LIFE IS FACTS ON A PAGE, YOUR ABILITY TO SEE THE ART OF LIFE IS LIMITED.

If you want to give your life meaning, tell yourself a good story about yourself. Story is the power to change your surroundings (context) and your meaning (subtext).

THE ART OF STORYTELLING IS A FRAMEWORK. IT'S AN APPROACH TO WONDROUS CHANGE.

THOSE WHO HAVE A 'WHY' TO LIVE, CAN BEAR WITH ALMOST ANY 'HOW'. - VICTOR FRANKL

The storytelling heart started as an experiment.

The catalyst for this experiment was pain.The pain was feeling so much potential within my self, friends and community but not being able to reach that potential. I had to start telling myself a better story, I also had to start telling others a better story. I would see people make great movies, make great music, build great companies and non-profits.

There would be a voice in the back of my head that would tell me, "You can do that too."

I would also hear a voice tell me to "Keep dreaming."

When you are serious about using the tools of storytelling to influence your life you will ultimately have to face the voice that tells you, "Stop because they will laugh at you."

I FOUND HELP IN AUTHORS AND
FRIENDS. YOU TOO WILL FIND
YOUR HELP TO FIGHT THE
VOICE OF FEAR IN FRIENDS.

MENTORS. AND IN COMMUNITY.

"YOU CAN'T TELL PEOPLE HOW TO CHANGE, YOU CAN ONLY INSPIRE CHANGE."

"I THINK THE MOST PRODUCTIVE
THING TO DO DURING TIMES OF
CHANGE IS TO BE YOUR BEST
SELF. NOT THE BEST VERSION OF
SOMEONE ELSE."
– SETH GODIN

With inspiration in mind, I sought out
how to inspire change for those who
seem stuck in a "status quo framework."

This book is a personal letter to my younger, stuck self.

This is the inspiration that lead me to change my world around me. This is my attempt to change the world. Yet all of this is still an experiment.

Fill in the blank with the most interesting / important thing in your life right now:

_____ IS ABOUT EXPERIMENTS.

When we change our internal narrative from:

"_____ is about perfection"

to

"_____ is about experiments"

our brains can now have freedom to explore the field instead of trying to be perfect.

When we do this our brains are allowed to think creatively instead of about processes and procedures. Our brains get bogged down in process and procedures and we end up paralyzed when it comes to facing our dreams. Even if we make incremental progress toward our dreams we feel stuck or slow moving. We often shut down because we are striving for perfection instead of really making progress.

We don't make progress for two simple reasons:

1. Lack of Clarity
2. Perfection

IN ORDER TO EVEN BEGIN WE MUST GO FROM AMBIGUITY TO CLARITY. WE MUST ALSO GO FROM PERFECTION TO EXPERIMENTATION.

LETS START WITH CLARITY.

I don't believe we can ever get 100% clear. There is never enough time or attention we can give to situations to bring total clarity. We can give enough time and attention to gain enough clarity. Enough clarity is all we really need.

Finding clarity is a daily task. Things change so your clarity will change with time, situations, and circumstances. This is a time consuming task. In our microwave society fast is what we seek. Clarity is a slow valuable drip of conscious information. You have to be willing to invest the time.

SO WHAT DOES INVESTING THE TIME LOOK LIKE?

The first step is gaining clarity **around your values.** We all value different things, so when you **articulate your values** you attract other people with the same values. This is important because you will eventually need others in your "Storytelling Life." Articulating your values will ultimately help you find collaborators, fans, clients and new friends. Be brave in articulating your values.

Here is where we start to get interactive. Grab a pen and fill in the following blanks:

WHAT ARE MY TOP 7 VALUES?

1. _____

2. _____

3. _____

4. _____

5. _____

6. _____

7. _____

BASED ON YOUR TOP 7 VALUES NOW ANSWER THE FOLLOWING QUESTIONS:

1. What matters most (to me) now?

2. What gives me energy and confidence?

3. What am I willing to accomplish today / this year?

4. How will this change the future?

These 4 questions are to get your mind picturing the future you want to build. If you are experiencing any resistance or boredom in this exercise, try and sit silent for 1-10 minutes. I know it is difficult but focus on your breathing. Inhale for three seconds, hold your breath for three seconds and exhale for three seconds. Do this until you have nothing rattling around inside your head distracting you. A good three minutes of silence will help you gain the clarity you need in any situation.

Answering these questions is crucial in order to change the current narrative, this is the foundation of creating a storytelling heart.

An action step in creating clarity in your story is...

WRITE A MANIFESTO!

A manifesto is a document that states your intention of change. It comes from the latin word "stretch to change." It is a great way to make a declaration of change, making a break with the past, and develop the new plot of your storytelling life.

Here is my storytelling manifesto. Hopefully it inspires you to write yours:

Time if finite. Love & passion are infinite. That is why we have such an internal struggle. Do what you love, often. Carpe Diem and don't let go. Share your thoughts, love & live life with others who care. Find a community that resinates with your core values and join the global community. Travel far; travel often. Don't look back. Help others. Tell yourself the best story about others. Inspire Change.

Live your favorite movie. If you get stuck: wash, rinse and repeat. Don't give in to the naysayers. Invest in life.

Now you may be thinking, "Really?!" (This sounds cliché.)

My answer to you is, "Yes!"

We are all trying to get to, "Happily Ever After." Yet if I were to ask you, "WHAT IS YOUR HAPPILY EVER AFTER?" You probably wouldn't have a clear answer.

More Money.

More Time.

A bigger _____. (Fill in the blank with any physical object of your desire. Saying a body part is childish...but yes it's funny.)

Gaining clarity starts with dreaming a full dream of who we are and where we want to go. Writing a manifesto gives you vision for who you want to be (subtext) and where you want to live (context).

Writing a manifesto also will show you the barriers to your personal change.

When we can get honest about the things we are afraid of, we step into a deeper place of self discovery. Beyond our fears lie the barriers of change.

Now it's your turn. Write your own.

MY MANIFESTO:

_____

_____

_____

_____

_____

_____

_____

_____

_____

_____

PERFECTION IS THE ENEMY.

"HAVE NO FEAR OF PERFECTION, YOU'LL NEVER REACH IT." - SALVADOR DALI

"HACKERS TRY TO BUILD THE BEST SERVICES OVER THE LONG TERM BY QUICKLY RELEASING AND LEARNING FROM SMALLER ITERATIONS RATHER THAN TRYING TO GET EVERYTHING RIGHT ALL AT ONCE. TO SUPPORT THIS, WE HAVE BUILT A TESTING FRAMEWORK THAT AT ANY GIVEN TIME CAN TRY OUT THOUSANDS OF VERSIONS OF FACEBOOK. WE HAVE THE WORDS

"DONE IS BETTER THAN PERFECT"

PAINTED ON OUR WALLS TO REMIND OURSELVES TO ALWAYS KEEP SHIPPING."

-MARK ZUCKERBERG

"PERFECTIONISM IS THE VOICE OF THE OPPRESSOR. THE ENEMY OF THE PEOPLE. IT WILL KEEP YOU CRAMPED AND INSANE YOUR WHOLE LIFE. AND IT IS THE MAIN OBSTACLE BETWEEN YOU AND A FIRST DRAFT. I THINK PERFECTIONISM IS BASED ON THE OBSESSIVE BELIEF THAT IF YOU RUN CAREFULLY ENOUGH, HITTING EACH STEPPING-STONE JUST RIGHT, YOU WON'T HAVE TO DIE. THE TRUTH IS THAT YOU WILL DIE ANYWAY AND THAT A LOT OF PEOPLE WHO AREN'T EVEN LOOKING AT THEIR FEET ARE GOING TO DO A WHOLE LOT BETTER THAN YOU. AND HAVE A LOT MORE FUN WHILE THEY'RE DOING IT."
ANNE LAMOTT

Perfection is sabotage. Seth Godin calls it our "lizard brain". Stephen Pressfield calls it *the resistance*. But you have to identify the fear that tells you not to accomplish your goal. The fear will tell you, "People will laugh at you." The fear will tell you, "Friends will leave you." The fear will tell you, "Chasing your dream is impossible."

I have found one way to overcome the fear is to let the fear lead you.

That's right.

If you are not afraid of ridicule, if you are not afraid of failing, if you don't fear wasting your time, then you are not really trying. You have to get comfortable with the uncomfortable in order to let the fear lead.

BEING BRAVE IS ABOUT LISTENING TO THE FEAR EARLY AND SILENCING THE FEAR WHEN IT'S TIME TO SHIP.

Seth Godin talks about "thrashing" in order to overcome the fear. You "thrash" (making large changes) at the beginning of projects, not toward the ship date. You also ship when you run out of time or money. This ensures you ship. Even if the product is terrible. Ship it. You will get better with time. Just send it out into the world as soon as possible!

Your dream is truly about experiments and not perfection.

Maybe you don't have a product or service but you know you want to do something or change something.

Experiments allow you to ship half baked products.

Experiments allow you to have fun searching for the right workout program.

Experiments allow you have fun making art, even if you don't understand it.

The market calls this the MVP or minimum viable product.

Psychology calls this flow; getting into a mental state of operation in which you are fully engaged. It's hard to find a flow state when you are aiming for perfection because you break concentration in order to judge your work.

Judge before or after you work, not during.

The bells and whistles are added as your audience and market grows. The beauty of your story will be added later. It's important that you start being curious.

Just do and perfect your story later.

Whatever your dream is do it and show it to people as fast as possible.

Don't wait, ship.

The world is wanting to see new art, new theories, new stories, new photos. If you love to do it, show it.

THE GUARDS AGAINST PERFECTION:

1. Ship an M.V.P.
2. Ship when you run out of money or time.
3. Identify the fear and silence it with early "Thrashing."

Use your core values, the four daily questions, and guards against perfection to continue to ship your passion.

CHAPTER TWO: STORYTELLING MIND

THE STORYTELLING MIND

Disney coined the term "Edutainment" in the early 20th century. They knew that in order for education to succeed they needed to mix it with entertainment. They understood something that psychologists would later call the psychology of play.

In order to educate people Disney chose not to film lectures or create slide shows. They decided the best way to access the human brain was to tell a story. A compelling story entertains and at the same time educate. This is powerful for a few reasons.

WHEN YOU START TO TELL STORIES THE BRAIN GOES INTO "UNARMED" MODE. YOUR BRAIN IS ALWAYS FILTERING INFORMATION ABOUT THE WORLD AROUND YOU. YOU MAKE CONSTANT JUDGEMENTS ABOUT TINY DECISIONS ALL DAY.

For example, *does this person approaching you look safe? Does that movie trailer look like something I would watch. Does this burger look fully cooked to you? Is that boy looking at me? Can I not turn in my homework and still get a passing grade?* Your brain is wired to keep you safe and your brain is constantly engaged in defensive thinking when approached with new information.

But when you are told a story your brain stops functioning as a defense mechanism and goes into observation mode. If a politician knocked on your door you would go through your decision making matrix to see if this person fits your demographic. Do they share my belief system? The moment he talks about guns, abortion, or pizza you judge him. Stuffed crust pizza?! OMG!?!

But if you were to hear a story, the portion of your brain that thinks about judging stops. Politicians can't get past the front door of your mind, but storytellers can come in and sit at the dining room table and you can't help but let them.

STORIES RESOUND WITH US. THEY STICK WITH US. THEY DEFINE US. IF YOU ARE AN EDUCATOR, MARKETER OR A PERSON WHO IS BENT ON MAKING SOCIAL CHANGE YOUR FIRST PRIORITY IS TO BE A BETTER STORYTELLER. IF YOU NEED TO DISSEMINATE INFORMATION TO LARGE AUDIENCES, MAKE SURE YOUR EDUCATION IS ENTERTAINING.

TELL GREAT STORIES.

One of my favorite storytellers is Bob Goff.

My friend Ryan met Bob Goff and asked him how he prepares for speaking events. His answer amazed me.

Bob Goff will tell 15 stories in 30 minutes intentionally. He breaks each story into 140 characters and places them on a spread sheet. An Excel spread sheet. Weird.

Why 140 characters?

That is the attention span of this current generation. You have to be able to communicate in 140 characters.

YOU SHOULD BE ABLE TO TELL 2 STORIES IN 4 MINUTES.

Bob Goff is an amazing communicator because he leverages stories and makes them tweet-able. His communication is memorable because at least one of his stories will resonate with you. His ideas are bite-size and catchy.

Love Does.

That is one of his biggest ideas and he presents it in only two words. Can you present your big idea in two words? Three to five words?

I challenge you to make your big ideas bite size. Story changes minds and markets.

PLAY IS A CATALYST

PLAY BRINGS JOY AND IT'S VITAL FOR PROBLEM SOLVING. CREATIVITY AND RELATIONSHIPS.

Dr. Brown, founder of the National Institute for Play writes, "Play is art, books, movies, music, comedy, flirting and daydreaming"

Name 3 Games you used to play as a kid:

1._____

2._____

3._____

Why was playing as a kid easy? Why is play as an adult so difficult?

"PLAY NATURE OVERRIDES CARNIVOROUS NATURE." - STUART BROWN.

"AMERICANS HAVE STRUGGLED WITH THE NOTION OF TAKING TIME OFF." IN FACT. SHE SAYS. WE HAVE 'A LOVE/HATE BATTLE' WITH OUR VACATIONS. BOTH WANTING TO TAKE THEM AND FEARING THE CONSEQUENCES. OUR DISTRUST OF LEISURE IS A LEGACY OF OUR PURITAN FOREBEARS. WHO KNEW THAT WORK. NOT PLAY. WAS THE KEY TO THEIR SUCCESS AND SAW LABOR AS A WAY OF GLORIFYING GOD. PLAY. ACCORDING TO THIS VIEW. THREATENS TO UNDERMINE BOTH OUR SUCCESS AND SALVATION."
HARA ESTRAOFF MARANO (PSYCHOLOGY. TODAY)

Fun is necessary to get unstuck. Fun is a necessary ingredient in your storytelling recipe. Play is the tool you need in your storytelling arsenal.

You have to be willing to play to tell yourself a better story!

TEN THINGS ABOUT PSYCHOLOGY OF PLAY:

1. Play allows us to explore new paradigms.
2. Play allows us to understand our current surroundings.
3. Play brings joy which is vital for problem solving, creativity and relationships.
4. Play allows others to connect with us via shared life experiences.
5. Play is a catalyst to great ideas.
6. "Gamification" is the play of life in marketing, daily tasks and team building. SCRUM workflow is a form of play.
7. Art, movies, music, comedy and romance all stem from play.
8. Play is appropriate for the workplace.
9. We were designed to continue in play past our adolescent life.
10. Flow is the result of play.

FLOW / GAMIFICATION

"A JOYFUL LIFE IS AN INDIVIDUAL CREATION THAT CANNOT BE COPIED FROM A RECIPE."
— MIHALY CSIKSZENTMIHALYI

Flow comes from a state of play. People find the most success when they have their passionate interests (Play / Flow) meet another persons need (the market place). This is where we see people like Bill Gates staying up days to code in the university lab.

Flow is the state of mind you reach when you are fully emerged in kick-butt activity and time passes you by. It fully engages your mind, body and soul.

There is a Netflix documentary called "Happy" that touches on the topic of flow.

FLOW, TO ME, IS THE SECRET SAUCE OF LIFE.

When in the state of flow tasks become effortless, enjoyable and euphoric. It's the place where you want to be everyday for 8 Hours at a time!

CAN YOU IMAGINE LIVING YOUR PASSION 40+ HOURS A WEEK?

The reason why people don't reach flow is because nobody is responsible for getting you to flow, except yourself.

Your number one goal is to identify things in life that bring you to the state of flow.

The second thing you need to do is to find, "Where does my flow state meet the market place?" It's with that information you begin to build a platform that keeps you in that flow state and allows you to meet market needs. The best entrepreneurs, the best storytellers and athletes took huge risks to create their own platform for flow (success).

The truth is you can't automatically jump into a flow state and hope people will pay you. You have to create a platform. Creating or leveraging a platform is about putting your content online. Making your story digestible, accessible and intuitive. Whatever comes from your flow state you have to share it with the world.

You have to ask yourself the question, "What do I love?" Then do it. Eventually, you will find a way to leverage it for the market.

Finding your flow starts with finding your passion. We have to drill down to simplicity in order to build a firm foundation on how your story will tell a better life.

FLOW IS YOUR INSPO.

Your flow should inspire others to do something or to be someone. Inspiration is another key ingredient to getting your ideas, stories, and dreams to stick in this age of oversaturated information.

My Friend Nils Smith wrote the book on Social Media for churches. He would always tell me there are only three posts to social media: Information, conversation, and inspiration. Data like time, location, policy, syntax are all information that we loose track of easily. Our eyes glaze over when we start to hear about tech specs, measurements of ingredients, engine specs, and other technical information, unless we have knowledge that transforms the information to story.

Questions are the conversation of social media. They are where things get really good on social media, but Nils would always say they are like stepping stones. Information and conversation are where everyone lives on social media. The real winner is inspiration. When you can inspire your audience you will be sought after, your social media pages will increase because you offer something that is at a premium.

Hope.

Your flow, your platform, your message, your hustle and daily grind are for one thing only: To increase hope in other people.

HOW DO I FIND MY PASSION?

There are two things that point to your passion. First is your bank account. What do you spend your money on without hesitation? Sports? Music? Photography? Technology? Food? Whatever you spend your money on is most likely your passion. Second is how you spend your time. What do you search the most of on YouTube or Google? Watch your "Recommended Videos" tab on YouTube because I guarantee they know your passion just as well as you do.

"-TAINMENT"

This new economy wants to be entertained, and that's not a bad thing. Stories, games, and cinematic sequences all fully capture our divided attention and make us focus. If you can get people to focus in this new economy you have already won half the battle.

TEN THINGS I KNOW ABOUT EDU-INSPO-TAINMENT:

1. Parables are stories that reflect a) culture b) our own identity c) the zeitgeist.
2. Public Service Broadcasters were doing market evaluations in 2000 and saw a trend toward market failure. Their

solution was to tell better stories cheaper, faster, and on multiple platforms.

3. Listen to a NPR podcast and learn.

4. Stories reinforce values.

5. Inspiration is ephemeral and expensive.

6. Tribes are the story of "Who I want to be."

7. Entertainment is the hardest portion of this equation because of budget, quality, and manpower.

8. Learn storytelling and leverage it in your business and marketing.

9. Darth Vader is Henry V.

10. The Wizard of Oz is a story of populism.

CHAPTER THREE:
STORYTELLING TENSION

EMBRACE VS RELIEF

I am a fan of Peter Voogd. He is a fast paced, quick talking, get stuff done kind of guy. I tell you this because I am the complete opposite. I'm analytical. I am reserved in my speech and pause to think about the next word in the middle of a sentence. It drives my wife nuts. My brain also works in this very weird way: I'll pause and think about what I am about to say and I have three other ideas pop into my head at the same time, so instead of pausing for emphasis, I just zone out.

Sucks.

Not Peter. His audio books, videos and podcast are full of charisma. I shy away from charismatic people because…..Really?! Sometimes too much charisma seems phony. Yet, Peter feels genuine in his communication.

TO ME CHARISMA CAN BE A DEFICIT.
THANKS TO JIM COLLINS' BOOK
GOOD TO GREAT FOR MAKING THIS
A MAIN POINT OF LEADERSHIP.

I also had horrible experience with a charismatic leader who was oblivious to the lives he was destroying.

That painful experience was enough to open my eyes to the deficit of charisma.

Not all charisma is terrible. But charisma tends to lead the conversation to a positive, happy place. When sometimes we need a very real conversation.

So why am I a fan of Peter Voogd? Because he is able to shift people's paradigms in a matter of moments. Literally. He is willing to talk about the unhappy place. Why? Because it's necessary in our storytelling journey.

In his book "6 Months to 6 Figures" he talks......HEY DON'T JUDGE ME BECASE I READ A BOOK CALLED 6 MONTHS TO 6 FIGURES. In his books he pushes people to not relieve the tension pain is causing you.

DO NOT RELIEVE THE TENSION PAIN IS CAUSING YOU!

I am not talking about physical pain, but the existential pain that messes with us. Peter claims this tension should drive you. We relieve tension by entertainment, alcohol, and escapism instead of tackling your next project. You see the storyteller is all about embracing tension in order to build a better story. If your life were a movie or book would people watch it? Do you think it would be exciting to watch you watching Netflix? What would be the most exciting thing to watch is a person who faces their tensions.

WE RELIEVE TENSION BY ENTERTAINMENT. ALCOHOL AND ESCAPISM INSTEAD OF TACKLING YOUR NEXT PROJECT.

THE STORYTELLER IS ALL ABOUT EMBRACING TENSION IN ORDER TO BUILD A BETTER STORY.

Your tension may be, "I want a better job" or "I need to lose 25 pounds." You may need to drop a bad habit or go to counseling for past trauma. You have to face the tension. Ignoring it, bandaging it, or trying to relieve it only makes the tension stronger. When the tension gets too strong it can feel debilitating. A good storyteller knows the breaking point of his or her character. It's better to get to your breaking point by embracing the tension vs. ignoring the tension.

IGNORING IT, BANDAGING IT, OR TRYING TO RELIEVE TENSION ONLY MAKES THE TENSION STRONGER.

The "dark night of the soul" is a film makers term. It's a plot device that usually shows our characters utter defeat in the third act of the film. It is the moment of defeat where the character looks his tension square in the face, and it defeats him.

Almost always the character has a solution in the next scene where secondary characters motivate him to further embrace the tension and finally apply the solution.

But the character doesn't do this alone.

IT WOULD BE WRONG OF YOU TO JOURNEY ALONE.

IT WOULD BE WRONG OF YOU TO THINK YOU CAN'T FAIL.

IT WOULD BE WRONG OF YOU TO GIVE UP BEFORE YOU REACH YOUR GOAL.

You need supporting characters when embracing tension. It's so important to have friends and family who will not let you off the hook until you solve the tension by embracing it. Community is our line of supporting characters in our "movie." The storytelling heart is quick to embrace the support of supporting characters, to find solace in community.

FALSE SAFETY

Many times we seek safety in the status quo. Family, teachers and coworkers will tell you get a good education from a prestigious university and find a steady job. Then, live below your means and hopefully you can fly under the radar for 40 years then retire. Then die. Where is the fun in that? I agree with education, I agree with living within your means, but that kind of life gives up a lot of control. Our education system is currently about standardization and not education. The same information you paid for is the same information the guy next to you is getting. There is nothing wrong with that, but higher education wants you to believe that you "now have a better opportunity" because you have a degree. To an extent that is true, but to another, millions of Americans have the same. We never differentiate ourself with academic degrees, we differentiate ourself with the value we add to others. Up-and-coming niche markets don't have degree programs. I spent two years in a job that didn't have a degree program because it was an innovative field that many people thought didn't have market viability.

In these cases education is definitely needed, but I would have to have waited 3 years for a University to write and approve curriculum for that specific job. I believe the answer is self-education.

SEEKING SAFETY IN THE STATUS QUO IS NOT SAFE!

Self-education is far more valuable for several reasons. First, you get to choose what you want to learn. This autonomous learning helps you zero down on our market niche. You will implement what you learn faster because science... for real! Dan Pink, in his book Drive, discovered the three root characteristics of the human drive. They are autonomy, mastery and purpose. When you incorporate these three characteristics in your self-education, your natural drive increases, making learning fun and getting you to a flow state. Let's be clear, I am not saying to not get a degree. I am saying a degree is a starting point, not the finish line. A degree is the ticket into the race. Your education must continue.

OUR EDUCATION SYSTEM IS CURRENTLY ABOUT STANDARDIZATION AND NOT EDUCATION.

One storyteller made a huge uproar about the perceived quality of education. Malcolm Gladwell spoke at a Google event and told the executives that a degree from Harvard and almost any Community College was identical. He called it "Elite Institution Cognitive Disorder" or how class rank determines your chances for elite STEM degrees.

What this boils down to is you automatically compare yourself to those around you. You don't compare yourself to people who are not close by. What we begin to do is compile an inner narrative based around the performance of others around us.

We start to tell ourselves a story of who we are in relation to other people. We compare our intellect, abilities, looks, and economic status which can damage our own perspective on self. The truth about education is the top 33% of the university graduates across America, perform at the exact same level despite having different intelligence, abilities or socioeconomic status. What Malcolm Gladwell is essentially telling us don't compare because they basically function the same. Some are just more expensive than others.

WHEN WE START TO COMPILE OUR SELF NARRATIVE, IT'S IMPORTANT TO NOT COMPARE OUR PERFORMANCE.

FEAR GETS A BAD RAP

The problem with fear is Hollywood. Hollywood places fear in a one-dimensional role in all of its films and it's usually a plot point to be overcome. When we look at fear in a Hollywood style, one-dimensional aspect, we ignore all the qualities of fear that can teach us or help us along our storytelling journey. Fear is a part of the way. So much so ancients used to tell one another, "Fear of the Lord is the beginning of wisdom."

Esoteric, right? How can fear be anything but paralyzing?

The answer is that you can learn from fear, you can draw near to great things because of fear. When we are admonished to "not be afraid", it isn't to steer clear of fear itself, but to not be paralyzed when fear shows up.

How do you allow fear to stay present in the car and not let it take the drivers seat? For me it's to keep moving forward. A very important lesson I learned about fear is I am not afraid of what I think I am.

I AM AFRAID OF HOW OTHERS WILL REACT TO MY INNER NARRATIVE.

There is this fear filled idea that if I change my inner narrative, and it doesn't align with what people think of me, I will not be taken seriously. People may think you are crazy when you set goals that are out of your comfort zone. People may start to judge you when you change your diet, your hair color, or religious preferences. Don't worry about them. This is when the fear gets loud. This is when fear says, "Let me take the wheel and I will take us back to a comfortable place" and not, "Let's drive down a path we have never gone before!" You have to live with the tension of nobody else believing your own inner narrative. This is good tension.

The naive person wants to silence the fear and as a result will become paralyzed and make excuses for their self-inflicted debilitation. Being "fear adverse" is one of the most dangerous things we can do.

Fear is a compliment to faith. It's the truthful possibility of all that can go wrong, yet it brings gravity to faith when you proceed anyway. Faith without works is dead, but sometimes it is the fear that propels us forward. It's the terrible odds that somehow inspire us. I am not talking about developing an inferiority complex. I am talking about sticking with a great inner narrative that allows you to face fear and to not let it control you.

Fear is an emotion, triggered by natural threats. This was great when there were animals looking to eat you for lunch. This was great when other hostile tribes were traveling in your area to steal from you. Fear was an amazing emotion that kept us alive in the wilderness. But technology has evolved and fear will not go away. And rightfully so. Technology and innovations are great, but as history teaches us Dark ages can come from great prosperity. The fear emotion will not leave the human race because it is a gift of protection. But in the current context of civilization we have fearful reactions to things that don't require the fight or flight response.

When you allow fear to drive, it will signal your brain to go into fight or flight mode and this mode is not conducive to reconstructing a new internal narrative. The trick is to stay with fear long enough to know it's an emotion. The perceived danger is not as dangerous as we think. When we come to a place where we can be in the car with fear and not allow it to drive, we becoming increasingly more powerful than we thought we could be. Stillness, meditation, and prayer are all ways to stay present in the moment and see your emotional narrative for what it really is.

If you want to try meditation and don't know where to get started, check out www.headspace.com for a good, guided meditation app. It's not at all what you think it is. It is not littered with mystical incantations or eastern philosophy. t is a practice of health. We will take a deep dive into why stillness is important in later chapters.

WHEN WE EMBRACE THE WRONG NARRATIVE TENSION

My friend wanted to be Holly Golightly from the movie Breakfast at Tiffany's. The comedy is very tragic and is meant to shed light on the feelings of inadequacy and loneliness. My friend wanted to be Holly Golightly, and I could never figure out why. The character was a gold-digging, mob informant who bounced from relationship to relationship and relied heavily on her looks and sexuality to bring meaning to her life. She was lost, fearful of life, and self-destructive to her self and others.

The book and film Breakfast at Tiffany's was meant to open our eyes to the subjugation of loneliness, the marginalization of those different from us, and what happens when we place our value in temporary things.

I was shocked when I found my friend started to live her life as Holly Golightly. She divorced her brilliant, handsome husband, tried her hand at modeling, and moved from large glamorous metropolitan city to the next. She abandoned her internal compass and compromised her values to get validation from men.

My wife and I were visiting one large metropolitan city on the west coast and found she was living there. We got connected with her to have dinner and she invited us to stay with her. It was such a nice gesture and we were happy to catch up, but once we sat down to have lunch she opened up about how miserable she was. Relationships have left her empty, the industry had taken advantage of her and she didn't know what to do. She was trapped, marginalized, fearful of life and in a self destructive pattern.

She lied. A lot. I wasn't upset that she lied to me and my wife, I was most concerned about her lying to herself. She followed the wrong tension of a narrative and she ended up like the character in the movie.

This alarms me because film is often meant to disrupt the status quo by showing the status quo's faults. By looking at the normal behaviors of our society it is meant to bring us to shock and alarm about the conditions we are living in. Sometimes we can't come out and say these thing because people will not listen, you have to Edu-Inspo-Tain them. But there is a possibility people will take the art at face value and not get the subtext.

You don't have to be that character; you don't have to follow the status quo. The comedy is really a tragedy, but meant to make us examine ourselves against the story. The problem is when a young, beautiful, fearful girl doesn't know her place in the world and see's a greek tragedy in the form of comedy and begins to resound with the character because she embodies the same traits.

Who is to blame her? Story is a powerful medium and if she doesn't get the subtext and context who's fault is that? Is the filmmaker responsible? Is the filmmaker a mirror of society or society a mirror of the filmmaker? I don't have an answer other than be mindful of the subtext and context. There is always a possibility someone will not understand the story you are telling, or the story you are trying to tell yourself. It reminds me of Jesus.

Jesus was a storyteller and many times even his closest friends and followers didn't get it. For example, he once said, "Eat my flesh and drink my blood." To that many people said, "Whoa! This is way too much." When you look and the subtext and context of the story, it is a critique of the current socio-political monster. The story becomes so powerful and rich in meaning when you see the subtext and the context. It helps you to identify the real source(s) of tension. Not what ostensibly causes tension.

When we pattern ourself after a narrative and we don't know our own subtext and context we can follow a path of destructive tension instead of tension that leads us to discovery and added value in life.

So how do you determine the correct source of tension? I believe it is found first in your purpose. Victor Frankl stated, "Those who have a 'why' to live, can bear with almost any 'how'."

The clarity comes from the calling of our purpose.

"THE NORTHSTAR HAS TO BE TRUTH." - GARY VAYNERCHUCK

CHAPTER FOUR:
THE STORYTELLING JOURNEY

What is the most epic story about your life that you wouldn't mind telling over and over again? You know, that story you tell at every cocktail party and gathering? Here is mine.

One time I was flying abroad, things were stressful and I was in a crazy transition in life. I had recently gotten sick a day before flying and I went to the doctor and he gave me a shot and prescription and told me to rest. I had an 18 hour day planned the next day. I was taking my family to Peterhead Scotland. Travel in the US was a breeze. The first stretch to the UK however got very difficult, very fast. I think I got food poisoning and having a sinus infection on top of that made my body do some crazy things. We missed a connecting flight and were flown to Heathrow to catch another flight to Scotland. I remember sitting in Heathrow and it was Patch Adams Day. Seriously, everywhere you turned there were nurses wearing red clown noses asking for donations. I felt weak, I was running to the bathroom every 2 minutes to dry heave and my wife and 2 kids were exhausted from the running around. I felt like I was dying.

My field of vision would narrow and I would stumble when I walked. We finally sat at a random terminal and I told her, "I need to go to a hospital, or a nurse's station." My wife was not having it. Suddenly a memory popped in my head. It was Matthew Broderick in Hawaiian shorts sipping a mixed drink saying, "Take some Pepto Bismol and get on over here." I found a shop in the airport and purchased a small bottle of Pepto and got on the plane. I know I sound like a diva, but I was pretty sure when we landed my body would have shut down. The flight attendants kept checking on me, I kept me head down and just had tears streaming down my face from the pain. What's interesting is I started to replay my life's events. I literally felt like I may not make it through the flight. Instead of playing all the best memories, something weird happened. I started replaying all the good times from the people who had hurt me worst. I don't know, but I feel that my mind was trying to reconcile an open psychological wound with telling myself a better story about people I don't like.

What's crazy is that brought so much peace to the situation. I was able to gain empathy and see life from their perspective. It brought me great joy to know they were just as hurt and afraid making the terrible decisions that they made.

WHEN WE EMBRACE A BETTER STORY, WE GAIN PEACE AND CLARITY BY REVISITING WHAT MATTERS, NOT SITUATIONS AND CIRCUMSTANCES THAT WE CANNOT CHANGE.

Everyone's storytelling journey begins with pain, defeat, or turmoil caused by not being aware in life.

PAIN IS ALWAYS AN INVITATION TO CHANGE.

Every time we experience deep pain or loss, time is necessary to reflect on the pain. Have you ever lost someone and then immediately thought about life? You thought about the moments you had with that person. You thought about how precious life is. What you were not thinking about is stupid stuff like the copier at work, or the bully in high school that called you names because of the way you dressed.

> "GRIEF IS LIKE THE OCEAN: IT COMES IN WAVES EBBING AND FLOWING. SOMETIMES THE WATER IS CALM, AND SOMETIMES IT IS OVERWHELMING. ALL WE CAN DO IS LEARN TO SWIM."
> – VICKI HARRISON

The principle of complementarity is an idea that light can act as a wave and a particle. Story allows us to borrow ideas from quantum physics and apply them creatively to our own life. We have the ability to blend the present sorrow with the present joy. This perspective is key to being able to start to tell yourself a different story. Complementarity at it's best is blending opposites.

Sadness and mourning are deep perspectives that invites us to examine life. Joy allows us to enjoy the examined life. They both have a place in the here and now. Emotions are what makes us present in our own story.

PAIN CAN BE THE CATALYST TO OUR "INCITING INCIDENT."

An inciting incident is a catalyst that wakes us up, or gives us the motivation to change. Every Hollywood movie has an inciting incident within the first 15 minutes. Timmy falls down a well; the plane crashes on a desert island. It's a problem of pain that sparks growth.

We don't have a Hollywood writer who can easily identify our "Inciting Incident." So we have to be the one to identify our own pain. We have to be comfortable talking about our pains, as existential as they may be, because talking about our pain will help us know where, what, and how to change.

PAIN MANY TIMES IS OUR WHY.

If your why for existing doesn't challenge some of humanities pain, then you may feel empty when you reach your goals and dreams because no pain has been challenged.

When you boil down you story to it's core, it will always be about someone overcoming their personal pain and fear to help others do the same.

> "ARE YOU AN EXTRA IN SOMEONE ELSE'S MOVIE SCRIPT OR ARE YOU THE LEAD AUTHOR OF YOUR OWN BLOCKBUSTER?"
> – CHAD COOPER

The Story Telling Heart is a framework for embracing the pain, taking time to evaluate what matters most, and to take the journey to the hard places you need to journey in order to go forward. Sometimes that means driving backwards into the pain, but ultimately it means taking ownership of your life.

Your life is broken down into a few distinct parts: time, energy, money, relationships, health, dreams, and personal development. The journey is about finding out what is most important to you. That is why we reset the problem solving loop by observing stillness or meditation for 10 minutes. This clears out the brain in order to give you focus.

FOCUS IS KEY.

Your inner narrative has been bombarded with ideas, thoughts and limitations from your surroundings, subconsciously. So taking the journey takes diligent focus and a strength to journey towards the inner narrative, rather than seeking external stimulation to distract from everyday life.

Your dream to build something, to make art, to change the paradigm of the current establishment all starts with an inner journey of why.

PAIN.

If you don't have a strong why, if you don't fully develop your inner story, at the first sign of resistance, you will quit. I see too many people talk a big game about how they are going to get fit, or marry a top model or go save thousands of people's lives in Africa.

We all have friends that believe they have no limitation and are God's gift to humanity. When our ambition is smaller than the tenacity of the problem, we are setting up for failure. Large ambition + small understanding = failure.

Once faced with reality will we shrink back and quit? Is our inner narrative telling us not to admit our failures? Ignore it? We all feel the pull of something more beyond safety.

FINDING "A WHY" THAT YOU WANT TO SPEND THE NEXT 8 - 10 YEARS WORKING ON IS KEY. THEIR ARE NO OVER NIGHT SUCCESSES. HARD WORK WILL ALWAYS BE HARD.

There are three formulas to help understand story basics.
1. Character + Conflict = Meaningful Outcome (Journey)

2.
Education+Inspiration+Entertainment=Attention (Edu-Inspo-Tainment)
3. Journey+Attention= Platform for change

Formula #1 is how we change direction in life. You may not be able to choose the family, coworkers, or socio-economic state in which you were born, but you can choose your conflict.

You have the ability to jump into a deep meaningful conflict that can change you and the world. If you are able to solve your problem, you are able to solve many problems.

Formula #2 is about grabbing attention. You have to educate without becoming boring or preachy. You have to inspire and still be based in reality.

Finally you have to entertain but not leave your audience empty.
If you successfully combine formula 1 and 2 you have formula for a personal

journey and recipe how to get people to come to you for answers.

IT'S THE RIPPLE EFFECT. IF YOU CHANGE YOUR JOURNEY. YOU SEND A RIPPLE OF POSSIBILITY INTO THE POND OF REALITY.

YOU DISRUPT THE NEGATIVE IDEAS, THE DESTRUCTIVE SELF TALK, THE VIBES THAT SAY "YOU CAN'T", WITH POSITIVITY OF AN ACTION THAT CHANGES YOUR TRAJECTORY FOR THE BETTER.

This will help us further embrace tension and fear in our journey. It's through these mental obstacles that we are refined in our character and ultimately become the person we want to be.

Fear can be tricky though. Since fear talks in half-truths we can easily become confused. Fear taps into the negative self talk, fear coaches self talk to sound positive, but still undermines us in our storytelling adventure. Fear tells the negative self talk to focus on circumstances. In this way negative self-talk is hidden under the radar. If negative self-talk was about self it would be easily detectable. So what does fear and negative self-talk do? They give you "fear goggles."

"Fear goggles" are a mechanism that keeps us stuck and stagnant. "Fear goggles" make your problems look bigger than what they really are. It's a brilliant strategy negative self-talk uses to keep you paralyzed. Negative self talk won't dare cross your ego by telling you things like, you're the underdog. That would help, because we are always up for a challenge. Negative self-talk will tell you, "You are more than capable, so when you fail everyone will laugh and think less of you." Truth is, not too many people will notice if you fail. Not too many people pay that much attention. But fear and negative self-talk target your ego. When you slay the ego and stay curious, you win.

Your ego is being fed lies about your ability and your outcome of failing. You have to fail, you have to take action and you have to let your ego take hits. It's like dodgeball. You think if you get hit by the ball it's going go hurt like mad, but the truth is the ball is 90% styrofoam.

ARE YOU AFRAID OF STYROFOAM? YOUR EGO IS.

That's why it's important to slay the ego daily. Don't make decisions based on your ego. Make decisions around your desires and dreams in life and fail toward those daily.

Yes, I said fail toward your goal.
The easiest way to learn is to do. The hardest part is knowing our first attempt will not look like what we envisioned.

It's ok, do it again. Stay curious and have fun.

You will come to a point where your failures will turn to success and people will admire your bravery and start to follow you.

You will come to a point where your failures will turn to success and people will admire your bravery and start to follow you.

CHAPTER FIVE:
STORYTELLING TOOLS

What do Abraham Lincoln and Steven Spielberg have in common? We will get to that in a second.

The Greeks used a word, Elutheria, to describe freedom.

ATHENS' CONSTITUTION IS CALLED A DEMOCRACY BECAUSE IT RESPECTS THE INTERESTS NOT OF THE MINORITY BUT OF THE WHOLE PEOPLE. WHEN IT IS A QUESTION OF SETTLING PRIVATE DISPUTES. EVERYONE IS EQUAL BEFORE THE LAW: WHEN IT IS A QUESTION OF PUTTING ONE PERSON BEFORE ANOTHER IN POSITIONS OF PUBLIC RESPONSIBILITY. WHAT COUNTS IS NOT MEMBERSHIP OF A PARTICULAR CLASS. BUT THE ACTUAL ABILITY WHICH THE MAN POSSESSES. (PERICLES. 431 BCE)

Storytelling and democracy have two things in common. You have to be able to communicate a language that the "whole people" understand. Every word or idea you communicate must bring a desire to pursue freedom.

A terrible internal narrative is one that thinks and communicates that "only I know how hard life is" or "people don't understand me."

The reason that narrative is unpopular is because it acts entitled, or disenfranchised, separating itself.

SEPARATION IS A STORY KILLER.

When we have a victim mindset, we look for ways to lose, knowing we may gain sympathy or attention for our plight. We have to reframe your mindset to understand a universal truth of the best story tellers.

We all feel pain, fear, and disappointments.

In comparison, your life may look like a Twinkie to someone else, but it's not the depth of pain that connects us but the presence of pain itself.

Don't believe me?

Why are we so attracted to stories of an underdog?

We can all relate to the main character's pain.

Slumdog Millionaire. If you are reading this book, chances are you didn't grow up an orphan who was forced into a life of crime in India. But the tension of a young man searching for love, fortune, and a chance to redeem his childhood resonates with everyone on the planet. We can all relate to the pain of wanting to belong. We tell the underdog story even when we are not the underdog. We are all looking for freedom in our own personal context.

WE ARE ALL ALSO LOOKING FOR FREEDOM IN SOME FORM OR ANOTHER.

Being American, or privileged, doesn't guarantee you will be free. Freedom is a strategic way of living. Freedom is the main ingredient in pursuing a Happily Ever After story.

Abraham Lincoln battled depression according to biographers, but never did he succumb to the internal narrative that he was alone. He experienced a spotty legal and political carrier. Most would consider his political life to be a failure.

Why did he keep going?

We can never truly know, but my speculation is he embraced the tension in his life. He wasn't formally educated until he was an adult. He was rumored to walk for miles just to borrow a book. He was constantly reading. He worked for years in manual labor, shop keeping, and didn't venture into law and politics until well into his adulthood. His political views were not popular during his time and he was always losing. He lost family at an early age, he lost relationships, children, and lost elections in politics.

Why do you keep going?

How could a tried and true "loser" be considered one of America's greatest heroes?

It was in his ability to channel his pain and failures to relate to those around him.

Lincoln's words and beliefs shaped the USA in one of it's most tumultuous times.

WHEN OUR PAIN IS SHARED IT BRINGS RELIEF THAT WE ARE NOT THE ONLY ONES.

This is huge!

When your story is filled with admitted pain, people start to gravitate toward your positive outlook on negative things.

THE BEST FILM MAKERS AND STORYTELLERS LEVERAGE THE NEGATIVE TO HIGHLIGHT A PORTRAIT OF POSITIVES.

It's paradoxical thinking, but that is the way the human brain works! Your pain can be a catalyst towards a better existence!

Many people think a great story is one with a happy ending.

A great story starts with points of tension, pain and failure. These emotions can build gratitude if we allow them too. Many times we become bitter, jaded and detached all because we carry the emotions instead of letting them be fuel to a passion.

When your passion is for others, your pain can easily be transformed into fuel.

If you only think about yourself in times of heartache, you will be alone and have only your emotions to guide you. This characterizes one of the best storytelling devices ever created that will help us transform our suffering / angst into fuel for good.

Your inciting incident of pain leads us to action when we think of others benefiting from our "Happily Ever After."

THE HERO'S JOURNEY LOOKS LIKE A ROADMAP TO A CHARACTER'S HAPPILY EVER AFTER.

The Journey starts with something called the inciting incident.

The princess is kidnapped.

The hero's family is tragically taken away.

The young outsider is bullied by a gang of blond social misfit karate models.

It's a painful process that awakens the hero's desire.

Here is a question to help you incite your storytelling journey.

WHAT MATTERS MOST?

"What matters most?" is one of those weird, funky questions.

Ask a friend, "What matters most?" and just wait for the reaction on their face! "What do you mean?" is a response you will get from somebody trying to swim in the ideology of "LET ME GET THIS ANSWER RIGHT!!"

Funny how there is no right answer to this question, but we all are engrained to be right.

This is a problem.

Wanting to be "right" is a problem because the answer you are willing to give is compromised with wanting to please the person asking.

School teachers teach us, "there is only one right answer." Our childhood teachers taught us they have the one right answer and to be rewarded in this life we need the one right answer.

The canvas of our mind has been painted by education to show us there is only one right answer. Having white space on our canvas is not allowing others to form our opinions or worldview. It's difficult to unlearn what society has taught us.

Opportunity is the white space on our canvases, and instead of using it to make something beautiful we cover it.

When in reality, it's our canvas. Shouldn't it be our choice to paint the future we want?

When you honestly answer "what matters most", you place a stake in the ground of what you want to accomplish, what you want to be, where you want to be and what you want to do.

Shouldn't we be able to choose and design the life we long for?

We will leverage the storytelling tools to help us build a vocabulary, imagery and patterns to follow so we can discover and journey towards our version of happiness.

YOUR VERSION OF HAPPINESS MATTERS.

We will clear our mental canvas of the previous images of failure, negative self talk, and paralysis that has kept us from moving forward. We will replace it with a great story that embraces our pains and failures and uses them as a fuel for a better story.

Clearing your mental canvas of clutter is a huge step in gaining clarity. If we don't calm the mental buzzing we run the risk of being paralyzed in our actions or giving up all together because of an improper relationship with fear.

I find that it helps to understand the functioning of some of the major parts of the brain that help facilitate clarity and non-clarity.

RESETTING THE PROBLEM SOLVING LOOP.

Our brains are a machine, literally. We can process 110 bits of information via our senses in microseconds. We are constantly making multiple decisions based on the information our brain is processing. Our prefrontal cortex is the language data center of our brain. It is evaluating situations and processing multiple outcomes of decisions.

But there is also a smaller part of the brain, called your amygdala. It's like your mean Uncle David that would always yell at you for not shutting the door fully when you go out side to play.

Jerk brain.

Your Amygdala is the same brain that lizards have. The software that the amygdala is running is basically "Brain 1.0" or "8-bit Brain." It is not so advanced. It's a basic human operating system responsible for pleasure, fight, and flight.

Things get sticky because the prefrontal cortex is basically an advanced problem solving machine that tries to see into the future.

Because we lived on earth as nomads and tribes the PFC helped us identify dangers like predators, other hostile tribes, and poisonous creatures. Since we don't live in such a hostile environment anymore, simple non-lethal things trigger the PFC in ways lethal things used to.

A pop quiz, social settings, a solo meeting with your boss, and a mean comment on social media can trigger the amygdala.

What's worse is that the jerk brain will constantly monitor your problem solving brain and without a moments notice hijack the entire brain function. This can lead to hostility, feelings of running away, and sexual fantasies that show up at the worst of times.

The amygdala "jerk brain" is where fear lives. Sometimes this fear is paralyzing. Literally. You may have a major decision or project you need to finish but you cant seem to start or finish it. That's fear driving.

It gets worse. Your problem solving brain is constantly looking for more problems. It will even invent problems if there are non to analyze.

This is why politicians can paint a narrative of turmoil and fear and society buys in. Our prefrontal cortex tells us we are smart because of all the problems we can find. It tells us we are safe if we are afraid and the jerk brain is more than willing to enforce the fear.

How do you expect to tell yourself a better story about yourself if you are constantly looking at the world's problems?

The "story hack" we all need to implement is something I call, "Resetting the Problem Solving Loop" Or "Clearing the Canvas of Mental Clutter."

There are many ways to clear away the fear and all have health benefits beyond the mental. Here are a few that will allow you clear the clutter.

MEDITATION

Meditation is probably the easiest to accomplish the goal with the quickest return. Taking 10 minutes to close your eyes and focus on your breathing works miracles.

Why?

When you close your eyes and focus on breathing you cut off the way the prefrontal cortex gets information. You are essentially starving the PFC from information. With practice the PFC quiets with activity. This may be difficult to start. Your mind may wander and you may start to think about other things. This is normal and a part of meditation.

I use an app called Headspace to help me focus on the process of meditation. It's also a very fun app to use.

Within three weeks scientist have seen the amygdala activity shrink in brain scans of people who practice meditation. Meaning fear literally shrinks.

This allows us to have a bias towards action. It allows us to be curious in our exploration of story and self.

JOURNALING

Writing is an extremely therapeutic way to gain clarity. Many people don't keep a journal because they don't know how.

Writing or keeping a journal shouldn't be terribly difficult. You can do whatever you want with a journal, honestly. Here are a few tips that help me in my journaling.

1. Make it a practice everyday. Grab a moleskin and just start writing. Write about your life, your childhood, your pain. Write about whatever. You can write about a coffee shop or why you

love country music. There is no wrong way to journal.

2. Try www.BulletJournal.com to organize your life. Again, just a suggestion, there is no right or wrong in journaling, but organization helps!

3. Keep a journal based around your passion for food, coffee, or your weight loss journey.

4. Draw, clip pictures from a magazine, or use a polaroid photo camera to document your life.

5. Use Evernote on your phone to journal digitally.

Getting the ideas on paper leaves space in your head for more important things. Journaling is key step to gaining clarity.

PHYSICAL ACTIVITY

Moving your body helps your mind tremendously. Just a twenty minute walk in nature can change your brain to lessen feelings of depression and anxiety.

Brooding, which is known among cognitive scientists as morbid rumination, is a mental state familiar to most of us, in which we can't seem to stop chewing over the ways in which things are wrong with ourselves and our lives. This broken-record fretting is not healthy or helpful. It can be a precursor to depression and is disproportionately common among city dwellers compared with people living outside urban areas, studies show.(How Walking in Nature Changes The Brain, Gretchen Reynolds, NY Times Well Blog)

Apparently walking in a park like area filled with natural vegetation helps us calm down. It helps stop the PFC's problem solving loop, or "Morbid Rumination", as fancy scientist like to call it. When you walk you lessen the flow of blood to the PFC and quiet the noise of life's what ifs.

"High Intensity Interval Training" is another way to quiet the mind. These intense plyometric workouts push your body to extremes and require blood to flow to your body rather than your brain. You literally have no energy to think about the repetitive motions because your whole body is fighting for oxygen and your brain is forced to release endorphins to ease the pain. After a HIIT workout you feel better and happier even though you are in a tremendous amount of pain. It's a lot of fun. And it hurts.

There are other ways of quieting the brain like laughing, a cold shower, or riding your bike through the nice part of town. Some methods work better than others, but what matters is the ability to start fresh with your storytelling journey. What matters is your ability to start your storytelling journey undistracted by fear. Try these techniques and keep track of how you feel after you practice them.

THE HEROES JOURNEY - PART 1

Structuring our lives like a Hollywood movie sounds audacious, suspicious, and filled with ego, but the success of Hollywood has been in its ability to tell captivating stories. When we live a captivating story, getting to happily ever after is easier than living in uncertainty.

The storytelling tools will not make you the next Kanye or Kim. The storytelling tools are not going to make you famous, they bring us to a place where we are fulfilled. Happiness is temporary, fulfillment can't be taken away.

What matters most is a question that helps us start.

Let's answer that question:

What matters most?

_____

_____

Your answer to "What matters most" should have three things all storytellers use to propel their characters forward:

1. Makes you realize your world is ordinary. Life right now may look like vanilla ice cream. Life may feel redundant or expected, something you wouldn't want people to write about in your autobiography. Wake up, eat breakfast, go to work, come home, make dinner, go to sleep. You have to come to a realization that your current state is ordinary, and you are worth so much more. You have the power to change the boring world around you. But it will take hard work and a journey.

What about your life makes you feel bored?

_____

_____

This monotony of living leads us to our second part.

2. Makes you feel called to adventure. You can now see a new horizon, a new adventurous world that you want to be a part of.

You want to travel, you want to make a difference, you want the space around you to change dramatically. And you have such a great time imagining the possibilities of change.

Do you have a Pinterest board dedicated to that change you want to see? It lives so beautifully on your phone, but what will it take to get your life to look like this?

Having a visual board helps keep us motivated in why we do what we do. I keep a vision board in Pinterest. It's a board that is filled with things I want to see for my life.

Part of my daily routine is looking at this board and reminding myself what matters most!

I highly encourage you to make a dream board. Fill it with the lifestyle you want to live. Incorporate viewing your dream board into your morning routine.

If a dream board doesn't sound like your cup of tea try making a dream schedule. How would you occupy your time on the perfect day?

6am_____

7am_____

8am_____

9am_____

10am_____

11am_____

12pm_____

1pm_____

2pm_____

3pm_____

4pm_____

5pm_____

6pm_____

7pm_____

8pm_____

9pm_____

Making a dream schedule shows you how you would spend your time. That is important because time is the resource that fuels your storytelling journey. If you don't have charge over your time making this journey will be difficult.

Take control over your time as soon as possible. We all have time commitments, but taking control is necessary in life. The way you spend your time will either fuel your call to adventure or it will drain your call to adventure.

When you have the time to pursue your call of adventure, that is called "curiosity." When you don't have curiosity that's called "an unwelcome time debt."

Some people kill their story before it even starts with the way they use their time.

Narrative is a very powerful way to engage attention. But there are some narratives that are not worth engaging in.

Television is a great invention and a horrible waste of time. If you are in

control of your tv watching habits, if
television grows your mental awareness
and keeps you curious to do the work
necessary, then that's a great use of tv.

If you are bored watching tv, that is
dangerous. Boredom is a way that
unwelcome time debt masks itself as
entertainment.

Your storytelling journey has to be filled
with a healthy balance of curiosity and
time management. I'm not saying be
busy or look busy.
Busyness is another way "unwelcome
time debt" looks to enslave you. If you
are losing sleep over your work, your life
or your projects you have potentially
purchased society's lie that success is
busy.

The storytelling journey is not about
success but about fulfillment.

It's important to remember your call to
adventure is not a distraction, it is a
destination in real life. Adventure leads
you to the third move of the heroes
journey.

3. You refuse to take the first step. We all face this in life. You feel inadequate, you feel under resourced, or experienced to make your dreams a reality. You become afraid to try and take the steps towards your dream. You fear failure, thinking you will lose your job, dignity, house, and have to sleep on a park bench.

When we answer the question What matters most, we start to feel the tension of "manifesto me" wanting to get to happily ever after.

We quickly see that we are not the manifesto version of ourself.

We quit when things get hard.

We avoid conflict.

We avoid telling others the truth.

We avoid acting on what we know we should act on.

So if we all refuse to take the next step, how does Hollywood get their characters to move forward?

How do the best business people, athletes, and successful people do it then?

The answer is this: we hack our story with external prompts that work in our favor.

We can't be trusted when it comes to getting started. So the most successful people take away the liberty of choice and place that in the hands of a coach or an experienced mentor, teacher, or counselor.

Have you ever heard of a mastermind group? They are a way people learn and work past the first three stages of the hero's journey.

Because of the current digital market, a lot of people are offering mastermind groups in exchange for money.

If you pay for a mastermind or not, that is up to you. What is most important is finding a group of people who fit your storytelling journey.

We all need to recognize this is "fear leading us." Don't be paralyzed by fear. We can sit on the sidelines because we refuse the pain of change or we can hack our story with the solution of getting past our own pain. The reason you need a coach or a mastermind group is they push you past what you are currently feeling and push you towards your goals. In essence, a mentor pushes you towards the first steps that matter.

THE STORYTELLING JOURNEY PART 2 - MENTORS, FIRST STEPS, AND T.A.E.

Step 4 - Meeting with a Mentor - There are two types of people who you need to place in your Storytelling Journey ASAP!

The first is the Mentor.

The mentor is a very important role in pushing past the refusal to take the first step. It's naturally engrained in us to take the path of least resistance. A mentor is someone that has journeyed the path before and accelerates your first steps to first victories.

Marty had Doc.

Daniel had Mr. Miyagi.

Luke had Yoda.

Jobs had Woz.

Who do you have?

Life is not a movie and the chances of you finding a real life Yoda are slim.

I tried.

Technology allows you to pick up your smart phone and find a mentor via the world wide web. There are books, podcasts, and videos that share some valuable insight.

I can't stress enough how readily available valuable information is in this day and age. The internet has made it so easy to learn and transform.

There are internet celebrities that are willing to share their knowledge, resources, and technology to help others.

When looking for a mentor, look for someone who is willing to help.

The question you initially want to ask your mentor is, "How did you do it?"

Sometimes this question is hit or miss. The heartache of finding this answer gets compounded when you don't have direct access to this person.

If you are looking for a mentor via book, podcasts and video here are a few helpful tips:

A.   Look for an experienced person in the domain you want to be in. I look to Gary Vaynerchuk, Seth Godin and Ryan Connolly as mentors. They are all practitioners and teachers. They have a determination to grow themselves first. They are not only great teachers, but learners who want to share their paradigm. Great mentors constantly add value by sharing their experience and paradigm. Look for people who can share their experience and paradigm. Philosophy can many times be noise if there is no practice behind it. Gary says it best in his video Clouds and

Dirt, "I don't spend any time in-between learning and execution."

If you need to start on a storytelling journey that focuses on health and wellness find people who have walked the path. While your path will be different, a mentor will show you the pitfalls are usually internal. They can see a bit further down the road than you can. Trust that. Respect that. And know a good mentor will allow you to fail! Why?! Because failing is part of learning.

B. Find a learning style that fits you. If you feel you don't have time to read or watch videos, I highly suggest podcasts and audiobooks. They are a great way to consume content while multitasking. You can listen while walking the dog, exercising, on your morning commute or cleaning house.

YOU CAN VISIT AUDIBLE.COM/ STORYHACKERPODCAST TO GET A FREE AUDIOBOOK.

But it's important to find your learning style. I learn best by watching someone do the task, then once I know the fundamentals I can improve or change and make it my own. Some people learn best by doing, others learn best by seeing or hearing. When you find your personal learning style you start to unlock something I like to call your "super power."

I was meeting at a coffee shop with a teacher friend. He is one of the most intelligent, compassionate and caring people I know. He told me his students all learn differently. He told me about one student who has a learning style of failing constantly, but when it comes to the ability to understand and execute once they learn, they are fantastic.

I stopped and asked, "A learning style of failing?"

The teacher explained that the student has to break the process, try other ways than the prescribed way and that many times leads to the project breaking and failing. But the student knows the material better than any other student in the class.

Our school system is failing her because every step along the journey is being graded. Her learning is being graded and coming up with the consensus of failure, but that is a legitimate learning style. After she has learned she can execute the problem perfectly. She isn't a failure, society has judged her learning style before she has actually learned.

DON'T COMPARE YOUR LEARNING PROCESS TO SOMEONES ELSE'S.

You may be wanting to talk to your boss about your ideas for work and are fearful. Embrace the tension. This is only the beginning. Just because it isn't easy doesn't mean you are failing.

Even if you do fail in every sense of the word, you are failing forward. You have made intentional steps towards learning, trying, and ultimately doing.

MANY PEOPLE FOCUS ON THE DESTINATION. THE LEARNING AND STORY ARE IN THE JOURNEY.

Embrace the tension. Learn from a mentor. Don't compare your path to others. Compare your path to "yesterday you" and the future "manifesto me."

C. Smart Journals win. It's best to keep track of progress, you should keep a journal of your storytelling journey. Write questions, progress, ideas and tasks in a journal to revisit to inspire you to reach happily ever after.

I use Evernote to track my progress; I use a Fitbit to track my steps. I love leveraging technology to give me information that I can then create a story from.

I found the days that I got in more steps on my Fitbit, were the days I was happier. The weeks that I had more than 10 listening hours on audible I was more joyful. My journal had the best notes after I had coffee with like minded people. The progress I was making was shaping the "manifesto me" into the real me.

These changes may be small to other people, but they can be huge to you if you follow them consistently.

The mentor will push you to further your storytelling journey.

The second set of people you need in your journey are allies.

Allies are different from mentors in the fact that they may not have the technical know-how to get you to your goal, but they are willing to support you however needed.

Many times allies are the people who will encourage us, push us, inspire us, and tell us the truth.

You need to surround yourself with people who you want to be like.

"YOU ARE THE AVERAGE OF THE 5 PEOPLE YOU SPEND THE MOST TIME WITH."
- JIM ROHN

Choosing a group of people who enforce the narrative change is imperative to getting closer to your version of happily ever after. If you struggle with the internal narrative, think of how much harder change will be if you are surrounded by a bunch of naysayers.

This is where we have to re-evaluate everything that influences our life.

Sometimes we have to burn a bridge with the negativity of the past to create a better tomorrow.

I remember waking up one morning thinking, "I am not where I want to be in life."

I hated my college experience. I hated the person I had become.

I decided to start fresh.

Anything that reminded me of my past I cut ties with. It was harsh.

New wardrobe, new music, new car, new apartment. Anything I could do to break ties with the past helped me reinforce a narrative that was healthy.

The best way to take action in your storytelling journey is to stay curious. Ask your mentor the following questions.

Quick side note. If you don't have anyone to call a mentor, I like the Think and Grow Rich method of mentors. Napoleon Hill was a huge proponent of master mind groups. He would espouse their mind sharpening effects in his writings. He even went as far as to assemble the greatest minds in history to meet with him and guide him. How did he do this? Hill used imagination to assemble his groups of Invisible Counselors. Darwin, Edison, Lincoln, Ford, and Carnegie were just a few of the counselors he would imagine and draw inspiration from. You may have to do the same if you don't have access to a mentor. If that is your case imagine asking your mentor or heroes the following questions:

What matters most?

_____

_____

How do you push past fear and
negativity?

_____

_____

_____

What was the best memory you have so
far?

_____

_____

_____

What are three tools that you wouldn't
be able to do your work without?

_____

_____

I am going to answer these questions for you from my perspective. There are no wrong answers to these questions. There are answers that will not resound with you. That is why finding a good mentor is literally finding a mentor that will fit your view of the world.

What matters most?

Freedom of time, choice, and resource. Adding value to others through my line of work that brings me and my audience freedom.

How do you push past negativity and fear?

Gratitude. I am also a huge practitioner of resetting the problem solving loop by practicing mindfulness.

What is the best memory you have so far?

The best memory in my personal life is at the age of 5 years old having a conversation with my father about honesty. It was the first time my parents had shifted my paradigm and I was grateful for the hard conversation and them trusting me at such an early age to understand integrity.

In my professional life it is always a conversation with someone who says my words helped them through a tough time.

What are three tools that you wouldn't be able to do your work without?

Empathy. Self-awareness. Ego.

Step 5. You cross the line to extraordinary. If you have embraced the tension, found a mentor and allies to help motivate and keep you accountable, you will start to see improvements. Having clarity on what matters most is key to your success and you will start to focus on achieving your goals.

There is a "secret sauce" of flow which we will cover in another chapter, but you will start to experience flow in the areas of life that matter most. Many times when you are true to yourself and your story, a flow state will make you feel like you are superhuman and can accomplish anything.

BELIEVE THE HYPE!

Being in a flow state is like finding your "super powers." Finding this extraordinary ability within you helps because you are about to face some really difficult "obstacles and enemies" in your storytelling journey.

HOW TO GET INTO A FLOW STATE.

Getting into a flow state is key to happiness and success. We think that success makes people happy. We think large amounts of money or notoriety will bring us happiness.

The truth is happiness is what makes people fulfilled and potentially successful. When you get into a flow state around what you enjoy doing, it should energize you. It almost feels like it's not work.

The trick is making sure you reach a flow state by following a few key factors.

In order for us to reach a flow state we need to find high challenging activity that requires high skill. Our brains can process 110 bits of information per second. A conversation normally uses 60 bits of information a second. In essence we need an activity that requires fine motor skills and in-depth cognitive attention. Activities that require large amounts of processing hacks our brain by pushing it to capacity. When we are at max capacity we don't have the processing power to think about our identity, our body's current state of feeling, or the passing of time.

Music, art, complex engineering or mathematical problems requires attention. You need to make sure that whatever challenge you are facing you have high skills for.

That is why being self-aware is so important. If you don't have the skill set for a complex problem, you can become stressed, apathetic, or bored. Those traits are story killers.

If you become bored or worried you can be assured that soon you will seek comfort in your old habits.

So how do you actually get into a flow state?

First I think it's important to define Flow psychologist Mihaly Csikzentmihalyi defines it. In 1995 a group of scientist studied the correlation between income and perceived happiness.

"INCREASE IN MATERIAL WELLBEING DOESN'T SEEM TO EFFECT HOW HAPPY PEOPLE ARE."

Even in cases where personal wealth tripled, happiness didn't increase. More money, notoriety, and fame will not bring you happiness.

Csikzentmihalyi studied the life of creatives and found when they are in a flow state they are most "happy" or in an "optimal state of being." Mihaly definition of happiness is when "the body or mind is stretched to it's limits in the voluntary pursuit of something ideal or worthwhile."

A flow state has 3 specific characteristics:

- Focus - you have the feeling that nothing else matters in the moment.
- Forget About Self - Not only are you focused but your brain doesn't even recognize the necessities of the body.
- Time Shift - you feel like time doesn't matter, but when you come out of the flow state you realize you spent more time than expected.

When you meet these three characteristics you are in a flow state. So you may be asking "How Do I Get To Flow?!?"

Getting to flow is not so much about what you do, but more about what you don't do.

Many times we need to resist the extrinsic motivations like money, success, fame and notoriety and focus on the intrinsic motivation that comes from our values.

Intrinsic motivations are the things that keep us going far past the promise of reward. It is the reason people keep going in life, that is made up from real substance, usually in the here and now. Like community, family, passion, curiosity, adventure, and discovery. These intrinsic motivations come from your values. That is why we create a manifesto from our values. That helps us extract the reasons why we work first. A sense of adventure plays into intrinsic motivation because you have the autonomy to choose your adventure. When you choose you are more likely to win.

When someone else chooses for you motivations drop and become extrinsic and not your own.

In Dan Pink's book, Drive, he sites Purpose, Mastery, and Autonomy as the three key factors that fuel people's personal drive.

When we incorporate these three factors into our work, into our storytelling journey, we start to develop flow.

Having autonomy is huge in incorporating a flow state. When we follow our intrinsic motivations we create a product, service, or story that is filled with intrinsic value.

Intrinsic value is a feeling of high worth toward what we are creating. When we feel high worth, the product, service or story we are forming will meet other people's needs we work harder than average.

So without further ado, lets set a checklist for getting into a flow state:

1. The activity has to have measurable goals and progress. You only grow in what you measure.
2. You must have clear and immediate feedback. Once you begin the activity you will know if you are near or far from your goal.
3. There has to be balance between the challenge of the task and the skills we possess.

Angela Duckworth author of "Grit" states that the people who are dedicated to the continual practice of a craft tend to experience flow in that craft. The flow state doesn't happen automatically, but over a period of time.

In athletics, the flow state many times doesn't happen until they are performance in competition.

Apparently you need to be absolutely committed to the task to experience flow.

Again that's why autonomy, intrinsic value, and purpose are all so crucial.

You have to choose your work. Other people will never commission you toward your dream. The details matter and being close to your dream but never actualizing it can be detrimental. Not only to you but the world who will never enjoy the creation you never created.

Art, science, discovery, writing, building, and cooking are all ways we can get lost in flow. The market is looking for quality and flow many times ensures quality because we care tremendously in our flow activity.

DON'T BE AFRAID OF BEING AFRAID.

I mentioned Bob Goff is a hero of mine. He constantly talks about how happy he is to get to a Thursday.

You may be asking yourself, "Why Thursday?"

Goff states that every Thursday he quits something. The thought is life is busy and in order for us to start something new, to keep exploring and discovering we need the time to do so.

In order to get into a flow habit we need to make time for flow.

Here is a helpful exercise: Create a stop doing list. Let's identify 5 things in life we can stop doing or delegate to someone else.

1. _____

2. _____

3. _____

4. _____

5. _____

Step 6. Test Allies and Enemies. The next step in your storytelling journey has been present your whole entire life. What is changing is your internal narrative. And whenever you introduce change you can offend those who are use to the status quo.

STATUS QUO IS ENEMY #1.

GREAT SPIRITS HAVE ALWAYS ENCOUNTERED VIOLENT OPPOSITION FROM MEDIOCRE MINDS. THE MEDIOCRE MIND IS INCAPABLE OF UNDERSTANDING THE MAN WHO REFUSES TO BOW BLINDLY TO CONVENTIONAL PREJUDICES AND CHOOSES INSTEAD TO EXPRESS HIS OPINIONS COURAGEOUSLY AND HONESTLY.
- ALBERT EINSTEIN

There are people who love the status quo. It pays them well. It makes them feel comfortable, valuable, and stable. Your decision to change will interrupt that. Navigating your growth in your storytelling journey is huge. You can inadvertently turn a friend into a foe.

Sometime people won't believe in you when you start your new journey. They expect to see the same old you. When you introduce someone to your "manifesto me" sparks may fly, they may ignore you or completely turn their back on you.

It's important that I remind you your storytelling journey is for others as well as yourself. Here are a list of tests you will encounter.

A. Your Manifesto Me Identity will be challenged.
B. You will come across a problem that your current ability will not be able to overcome (alone).
C. The Status Quo will give you a reason to revert to the old you.

WHEN YOU BELIEVE IN SOMETHING YOU ARE WILLING TO CHANGE YOUR LIFE FOR, BE PREPARED WHEN THE STATUS QUO LASHES BACK.

One of my favorite philosophical quotes is, "Our fight is not against flesh and blood." It's a parable to remind us that if and when we resort to violence we only attack the symptom and not the root of the problem.

The root of the problem is deep within the story we tell ourselves, about ourselves, and the others around us. We change story with story. We never change the story with violence. Violence is a last resort for self-preservation. When violence comes out as a first response we have already lost the war. We have lost the war within and have perpetuated the enemies story of "we are an enemy."

We overcome with a narrative change. Psychologically that may be a move in location, diet, attitude, the way we dress, or the way we address our problems. When we talk about fighting we are talking about fighting the ideas of old self, of the status quo and the misunderstandings of Manifesto Me.

The next part you won't like...ever.

CHAPTER SIX:
STORYTELLING ALLEGORY

I accidentally made a documentary once.

I helped a friend document his dream vacation.

Mike Andrews is not like anyone you will ever meet in your life. He is unassuming, sharp, and has a sense of humor that makes everyone laugh. You would think he is just a fun loving guy.

While it's true he loves fun, Mike is deep. Like a philosophical genius. His words are poetic and you can see in his eyes he truly lives them. While Mike would say he is a youth pastor at his father's church, he is a modern advocate for human rights. He is currently running a campaign to rescue two children from the Ukraine.

Mike is amazing because he doesn't let fear paralyze him. He doesn't let the word "no" define what he can and can't do.

For his son's birthday Mike wanted to take a trip to Ann Arbor, Michigan. He wanted to see a college football game with his son. Really simple idea, but a month before the scheduled trip an unexpected medical bill came up and all the money he saved for the trip went to pay the expense.

He was about five weeks away from a trip he had promised his son and had no money. Mike called me and asked what could he do to make the trip happen. We met at a coffee house and discussed his options.

I told him try and get sponsorships from sports brands and document his trip on all social media.

He asked about Kickstarter and if that would be a better option. He wanted to crowd fund his trip and in return he would show a documentary movie.

Mike met his Kickstarter goal and took the trip. I suggested he take a camera and take as much video as possible. When he got back we set up a time to do some sit down style interviews so he could explain a bit more about the trip.

In total it took us about 6 months to complete a short 45 minute documentary movie. Mike and I were both leery about the movie. We both felt the film was too long and not compelling enough. I enjoyed bits and pieces of the film, but it needed something more.

Opening night came in late December of that year. I am not one for self-promotion so I didn't tell to many people about the film. Mike rented a movie theatre for the night and premiered our film "AnArhBar."

That night we found our missing ingredient.

Story Step #7 - The Approach is about sharing your pain in a socially acceptable way that does three key things.

1. Pain captures the attention of your audience - They say, "Me too!"
2. Your audience leans in wondering if you found a solution - They ask, "What did you do about the pain?"
3. Your audience asks how YOUR solution fits in THEIR life - They ask, "Will their solution work for me?"

The key to success is sharing your pain in a socially acceptable way. The market doesn't want to hear your woes unless it helps them fix a problem. I understand times we need to share our frustrations and anger, but don't do that in the market place.

The Storytelling Heart is about taking the pain and transforming it into story solutions.

This, in turn, activates other's stories. It's great to have mentors and allies on your side, but your story should inspire people to take steps.

This means inspiring them joining you in your quest, helping them see their quest, offering a product, service, or solution. The market is a storytelling machine; The best stories are attached to the products that deliver transformation.

Step 7. The approach - Once you have gained confidence in yourself, you have a solid team, and a mentor to guide you, now begins the approach toward tackling bigger obstacles. This is a major challenge that neither you, nor your team, nor your mentor can face alone.

I love design. There is nothing like using a product that works well, looks good, and feels good. I have used products that may work but don't feel good or look good. Design takes the function of a product and marries it to form and aesthetics. Even hough we think of good design as a bonus, we sometimes forget good design can solve life and death situations.

My daughter, Emerson, was born premature and needed to be placed in the NICU for 2 weeks. It was a scary process. Emerson had low birth weight, her lungs were struggling to get her adequate oxygen, and she would shake uncontrollably. My wife wasn't able to see her for 48 hours because of health issues. I had to juggle work, caring for our 2 year old son, hospital visits, and checking in with nurses for my wife's and daughter's health. Life was exhausting, scary, and frustrating. Luckily we had insurance, First World medical care, and family to help us through the process. What would have happened if we didn't have access to that kind of care? Honestly, my daughter probably wouldn't be here today without the NICU, technology, and doctors.

Some students at The D-School and IDO designers decided that their storytelling journey needed to use design to save lives in Third World countries. Their problem was the infant mortality rate is staggeringly high among premature births in Third World countries. The machines used to monitor and heat premature babies is expensive, it's not portable and requirers education in order to understand the beeps and numbers it displays. These are barriers to entry for impoverished woman in India and other third world countries.

The design team at IDO and students at the D-School understood the pain of pregnant women in Third World countries. They designed a baby sleeping bag that would keep premature babies temperatures high. The baby sleeping bag had a pouch that could house a pouch of "phase changing materiel" that keeps a constant temperature for hours. This was the easiest most effective design solution that would keep premature babies alive. It was cost-effective and the technology was easily understandable. Women would heat the pouch and place it in a compartment of the sleeping bag. It took a team effort, an understanding of pain, and a group of brave students to tackle one of the worlds most overlooked problems.

When you form your storytelling team (the people who are encouraging you to pursue the manifesto me) you have the option of tackling major problems that the world faces. Some are life and death, others are simple, fun ways to bring joy back into people's lives.

When Mike Andrews and I premiered our documentary movie, we found our missing ingredient was people. People needed to interact with the story, they needed to take it and make it theirs. Mike waited 22 years to fulfill his dream, his pain of wanting to experience an Anarhbor football game with his son may seem trivial to you, but to a bunch of friends in a movie theatre that was a magic moment.

Everyone has dreams, Mike, in his bravery, shared his pain and the audience leaned in and said, "Me too!" Money is an obstacle for many people, again the audience leaned in and asked, "What did you do?" Finally after hearing the solution everyone in that room asked, "Will it work for me?"

That night Mike showed a documentary about playing catch with his son and how going to a football game could be transformational. That audience picked up on something completely different. They watch their friend, Mike, be brave.

THE STORYTELLING TOOL OF THE APPROACH IS TO BUILD BRAVERY IN YOUR AUDIENCE.

The story of you overcoming your pain brings people out into the open of vulnerability and strength. It's important to deliver on your promises, because if you take someone out of their comfort zone you need to be able to deliver on transformation to strength. If not, you could leave people hurting, or disillusioned about your product, service, or story.

After the movie, I had several people come up to me and say I had inspired them to take a risk on their dreams.

What?!

I didn't do anything other than bring a friend's story to light. That night I had a musician come up to me and say thank you. A year later he created a beautiful album that has inspired others. That night a veteran with PTSD, named Buddy, confessed he had been deeply depressed. He said he realized his calling in life was to take other Veterans with PTSD hunting and fishing in the great outdoors. It has been a hard road for Buddy, but he has lead a few veterans on excursions and helped them tell a better story about life.

You will never know the impact your approach to problems have unless you go for it. You must take your approach!

The people you find on your Storytelling Journey will sometimes surprise you. They may seem like they wouldn't fit your circle of friends. Don't discount the perspectives of those around you based on a different metric of life. When you find a Storytelling Ally don't push them away because of differences. If you want to watch the film go to: www.vimeo.com/191104289

This is a side note rant, but society teaches that we need to like people, in order to work with them or be friends with them. While it may be fun to work with people you love and care about, you only need two things to make a friend. You need to listen and to be empathetic.

Biases jeopardize our storytelling journey the most. Our biases are like warm, fuzzy blankets along the cold, weary path of self discovery.

We are using story for self-discovery and sometimes what we discover is we are not as "good" or "compassionate" as we think we are.

We fall into a system of thinking that limits our reach, limits our impact on others, and limits our own storytelling journey. Yet we use the storytelling tools to tell ourselves a good story when it's not appropriate.

I feel that success comes when we flip the narratives of

"I'm great at _____." to
"I need to work on _____."

and vice versa.

This helps build positive emotions around change and negative emotions around the status quo.

Why is this important?

Because culture, technology and society is changing ever so dramatically. When we get into a mental position of keeping the status quo we get stuck.

The reason we are taking this journey is to get unstuck, to discover our pain and share it because pain holds life's answers.

**"LIFE IS PAIN. ANYONE WHO SAYS DIFFERENTLY IS SELLING SOMETHING."
-WILLIAM GOLDMAN**

Step 8. The Ordeal - The reason good story structure in movies resounds with us is because we can relate. In the middle of every good story is a very big obstacle that could mean life or death for the character. It usually involves facing fear, leveraging your superpower and coming up the other side different.

You can't force an ordeal in your personal life. You could but... that would be the act of a sociopath. You don't want to create life and death ordeals in your life, but what you can do is leverage the story structure of ordeal to propel your current storytelling journey to happily ever after.

How?

There are two very important outcomes from the ordeal step of the journey.

The ordeal should change you. This change is solidified in facing a life and death ordeal. How do we experience this kind of life change without having to go through the process? We listen to other people's stories. This allows us a paradigm shift without having to go through the ordeal.

How does that work? Our brains sympathizes with other's stories, so when you hear someone else's story you feel the emotions they are feeling. This is how sympathy works.

Pain shifts the way we see the world. When you hear stories of pain and how fundamentally wrong we get life by thinking of problems in easy to manage packages, we lose touch with the world around us. The ordeal helps open our eyes to the problems around us.

When our eyes are opened to the world around us, we start to become valuable. We become valuable because we start to speak the language of those around us; We start to tackle problems from a different perspective.

The ordeal is a gift that allows us to change paradigms to overcome problems in new creative ways.

The ordeal is meant to make us brave and give us confidence in the midst of fear. Confidence is a tricky thing. Especially when you introduce social anxieties into the mix.

If you haven't adopted a way to deal with fear you need to.
In part one of this book we talk about resetting the problem solving loop. You will be stuck in analysis paralysis if you don't have a dedicated way(s) to face fear on a physiological level.

Another way we can improve our confidence is to do what we say. We lose confidence when we say we are going to do something and not do it. We subconsciously set ourself up for failure. It gets easier to quit once we have already quit along the way.

When you add the benefits of becoming valuable to bravery, your super powers now have an outlet. Your outlet is for other people. I encourage you to answer the following questions:

What is a major pain point I have found a solution for?

_____

_____

_____

What pain am I hearing from those around me?

_____

_____

_____

Step 9. The Reward - This is the step in your journey where you find your efforts pay off. All the work, fear, tears, criticisms from team and mentors build to your reward. This is not happily ever after, but a major step in that direction.

When approaching the reward phase of your storytelling journey you will notice something about how you feel towards the reward. Before, when you imagined your pay off coming, you were excited and expected the feeling of euphoria to rush in. Now that you have worked hard, taken criticism, made friends and enemies the reward almost feels normal or expected.

While still welcomed, the reward is more expected than cherished. This can be a major pitfall in your storytelling journey. If you stop at the reward you will miss out on the best part of your journey. You have to make the storytelling journey a regular part of your life. If not, you run the risk of losing your reward.

The rest of the storytelling journey is to help you solidify your reward, your community, your friends, and keep your "superpowers" sharp. This is a great point to celebrate but this is not the end. We must keep pushing forward in our journey.

What does giving my solution to other people look like?

_____

_____

_____

Step 10. The Road Back - Coming full circle is a theme of many stories.

After we have received our reward it is important to think about others. When you shift your internal narrative from being "all about me" to "how can I help" you become more.

You become more valuable. More compassionate. You become a better person. But thinking about others is not about becoming a hippy dippy, bleeding heart hero.

THE REASON WE COME FULL CIRCLE TO HELP OTHERS IS BECAUSE IT ALSO 'SEALS' OUR REWARD.

When we began to teach the storytelling formula to other people we learn it quicker than studying it by ourself. When we give and encourage others to overcome the fears that we have overcome, it solidifies the success in us. Not only do we know how to overcome obstacles or fear, but we have the power to show others; To help others to see them get to their happily ever after.

The road back is where you become a hero and a mentor. The best thing you can do is codify your process. The hero's journey is a to codify the process itself. It is a set of steps that can be modified and tailored to a variety of needs. Psychology, leadership, marketing, writing and communications all benefit from using the heroes journey.

Can you write down 3, 4 or 12 steps that helped you get this far?

What was the hardest step to take and why?

What step helped you learn the most?

Answering these questions helps give your "reward" to others. We love processes because they give action to ideas. Your tribe will benefit from you codifying simple steps to help them make progress.

Step 11. The Resurrection - When we cross back over toward "normal living" we face another dilemma. A big dilemma will be the way we want to return to "normal patterns of living" when we step back into life after our journey. The resurrection is all about how we can live with the tension of normal life never being the same.

Resurrection stories are about facing reality after doing the extraordinary.

There is a story of a resurrection of a Jewish Rabbi. He told his followers about his death, burial and resurrection. While being met with plenty of opposition from his followers, his enemies and his government, after his execution he rose from the grave, in a garden, on the first day of the week.

One of his followers went to mourn him and prepare his body for a proper burial. When she encountered the resurrected rabbi he told her, "Don't hold on to me."

That's a strange story. But what resounds about the story is how we are so quick to hold on to the past.

WHEN WE CATCH A GLIMPSE OF THE PAST WE ARE SO QUICKLY TO ABANDON THE IDEALS OF OUR MANIFESTO. WE SUCCUMB TO THE TEMPTATIONS OF FORMER HABITS.

The hardest part about the resurrection portion of our storytelling journey is we have evidence that the old "us" is gone. And with the passing of the old us, familiar, happy, fun things are also gone. We can get caught up in the romanticism of the past and mentally erase the pain, tension, and problems our old way of living gave us.

To fully live in the resurrection we must focus on what is alive in front of us right now.

This is where the Storytelling Heart gets confusing. In some cultures the happily ever after story is about poor people gaining the world. In other rich countries, it's about a rich person seeking enlightenment and / or loosing all worldly possessions.

You may be at the portion of your journey when success has been easy, or at least it has been with you for a while. But the things you are successful at are not in your happily ever after. At this point in your journey it is entirely ok to say, "I am on the wrong path or I have another journey to complete." The Storytelling Heart is a cycle, it is not a one time, fix all for our problems.

You will find the problems you began with, the tension about life, is now resolved and in its wake is a whole new set of tensions, problems, or activities that need your attention.

Step 12. Happily Ever After - Getting to Happily Ever After is difficult for three reasons. One is because happily ever after is not only for yourself. You must win for other people. You must understand your journey is to teach you how to overcome and you are obligated to teach others.

Second, happily ever after can be anti-climatic. The best part of your storytelling journey is the ordeal or the resurrection, the part where you are in the most conflict and where you are winning at our goals. It's where you have allies and mentors who are willing and care. It's those moments that make the Storytelling Journey worth it. It is absolutely about the journey and not the destination. Knowing this you are probably going to want to tackle another round of The Storytelling Journey. That's ok. You should use this template to map out your next storytelling adventure.

Finally, Happily Ever After is a fairy tale term. Fairy tales are allegories. Allegories are stories that teach us something about our surroundings. Many time parables, fairy tales, and comic storylines are presented to us without any definitive subtextual meaning. No one is telling you the scarecrow in The Wizard of Oz is supposed to represent farmers of America. No one says the cowardly lion is the political engine of the USA. You have to gather this information separately, from study and deep analysis. My hope is that you have the tools necessary to know allegory is just as powerful as math, science, engineering or medicine. The fantasy speech is sometimes the only language we know how to use when describing our ideal. The tension will always be there between the real and the ideal. Our job is to formulate the best story of how we can make our reality more ideal.

My hope is you are constantly willing to take the hero's journey again to reach another "Happily Ever After."

CHAPTER SEVEN: PUTTING IT ALL TOGETHER

"IF YOU SPEND TOO MUCH TIME THINKING ABOUT A THING, YOU'LL NEVER GET IT DONE."
- BRUCE LEE

"AMATEURS SIT AND WAIT FOR INSPIRATION, THE REST OF US JUST GET UP AND GO TO WORK."
- STEPHEN KING, ON WRITING: A MEMOIR OF THE CRAFT

Studies have shown that your brain is underwhelmed with social media. The flow state comes to those who are willing to engage in the hard, technical work. The pings from your phone have such a powerful draw because our brains are programmed to crave the release of the dopamine that attention gives us.

The flow state is key in creating a good life, but like many great things there are fake, cheap alternatives. Social media is a fake, cheap alternative to the flow state and deep work.

When we actively engage in the flow state we create and have a loss for sense of time. Adversely, social media, television, books and even education can be a loss of time if not practiced mindfully. Instead of creating in a flow state, we move into entertainment mode and times passes us by, yet we miss out on the flow experience and the productivity that comes along with flow.

Why am I telling you this?

TIME IS LIMITED.

Yesterday I was watching a Facebook live broadcast of one of my favorite communicators. He mentioned to his community that the doctors had found cancer in his body and it has been aggressively growing for years. Hearing the news was heartbreaking, but he had determination in his eyes and inspiration in his words like I have never seen in him before. How can this person be determined yet not having control over his life? I believe the answer is found in his storytelling journey.

I have found such solace in the storytelling journey because it takes into account that one day it will all be over. How do you want to be remembered?

Action is our friend when it comes to completing our storytelling journey.

In the past chapters we have looked at multiple tools that allow us to change our paradigm when it comes to our internal and external narrative. While these tools will make for a better life, the best way to use them is in conjunction with each other toward a specific goal.

I have structured The Storytelling Heart process in three acts. Act one is the "Problem and Self Discovery" phase. Walking through the four steps in act one help us declare "Why Our Journey Matters!"

Act two is the "Change and Resistance" phase. Again when we walk through the four exercises we are going to be able to declare "Who We Journey With!"

Act three is the "Share Your Gift, Gain and Glory" this is the phase where we declare "Where We Journey To!"

ACT 1

Step 1 - Identifying Manifesto Me (We See A Problem)

Step 1 is identifying the "Manifesto Me." When we drill down to our core values, when we express who we want to be tremendous possibilities open up. We have an idea of who we want to be in our head. When we get clear around the kind of person we want to become things get easier.

You may be asking, why not just set a goal? Why not start with a problem we face?

I think there is a huge misconception around success. We have come to associate success with our ability to achieve, yet when we look at happiness achievement only influences 10% of our overall happiness. If you focus on achievement you will only be about 10% happier. Starting with achievement first ignores the other 90% of what makes us happy. If we focus on the first 90% of what makes us happy achievement becomes way easier. 50% of happiness is temperament, or resting condition of our internal narrative. The other 40% is shaped by our actions and decisions.

The big thesis for Act one is let's identify the big 90% of happiness and start from there.

Step 1 is the manifesto me because it is a great kickstart to show us how our current internal narrative is failing us. Truth is, if you are the person you want to be right now then you have no need for this book. But if there is an inclination that life can be better, start. Start with the person you want to become.

Do you want to know why so many people fail at there goals?

It's because they set goals they can't reach and blame themselves for their failure.

SMART PEOPLE SET ASPIRATIONS TO DEVELOP **THE CHARACTER THAT IS NEEDED** TO REACH THE GOAL. THE GOAL IS ARBITRARY. THE CHARACTER IS THE SECRET SAUCE TO ACHIEVING GOALS.

The goal will come and go, but the character you develop in order to meet that goal will not leave you.

Having a manifesto that is based on your values helps you develop the character needed to become that person.

I know sometimes our "manifesto me" looks way different from who we currently are. That's fine, but don't become discouraged around the fact there may be a huge difference between your current context and the life you hope for.

Step 1 is about identifying. You have to remember that this journey is about fulfillment and not achievement. You will achieve, you will be a productivity master, but we don't start there, that is where we finish.

Step 2 - Questions to Ground Us (We Name Solutions)

Now that we have a pretty good idea of who we want to be, esoteric right, lets look at one key idea that will propel us into our storytelling journey.

Many authors have espoused the benefits of having one priority. Scientist have also found that we can't multi-task. Our brains act as if they are drunk when we juggle multiple tasks at once. We also screw up our ability to stay mindful in multitasking. Multitasking also collapses the ability of Flow.

Step 2 is about clarity, mindfulness and singular focus.

THE BEST CHARACTERS IN MOVIES ARE THE ONES THAT HAVE ONE SINGULAR FOCUS.

Why?

Because the audience can clearly identify the motives of the character, this is important because we hate wasting calories on thinking. The same is true for us, if we don't have a singular focus, confusion can set in real quick.

When we have a singular focus we can then filter all our ideas, thoughts, feelings and tasks through this lens and evaluate what deserves our attention and what doesn't deserve our attention.

For me that is a question that "centers" me.

My question is "What Matters Most?"

You can have a completely different question that fuels your clarity.

Some other great examples are:

"What does my art mean?"

"How can I make a change today?"

"How can I heal the world?"

"What makes me happy?"

The power is not in the question ITSELF, but in our ABILITY TO QUESTION OUR SURROUNDINGS.

When we are able to question our surroundings we are able to take note and make changes.

These questions are meant to show you a truth.

Here is the secret you have been waiting for.

YOU ARE POWERFUL.

These questions recognize your ability to act in your situation. Not only to act, but to do so mindfully and with purpose. take into account the here and the now, as well as the future. You have power in your decisions, so you might as well take this question slow and find out what propels you toward your happily ever after?

Step 1 revealed the problem, the tension between our current condition and where we want to be. Step 2 helps us gain clarity around the possible solutions to become who we were called to be.

It's important as we answer the question, we do it from the context of our manifesto me. We think about how would our "best self" tackle this problem.

I encourage you to find your question and answer that daily. Answering the question daily will help create momentum toward your happily ever after, the momentum you gain will be in the right direction because they stem from your ideals and values.

"SUCCESS IS THE GRADUAL REALIZATION
OF A WORTHY GOAL OR IDEAL."
-EARL NIGHTINGALE

YOU ARE ON THE RIGHT PATH.

Step 3 - Resetting The Problem
Solving Loop
(WE GAIN CLARITY)

Your brain is your biggest asset, but is
also the source of a majority of the fear
and failure in your life. Fear of success
and failure all steam from two narratives
that collide in our brain. The internal
narrative, or our self talk, paints a
picture of how we see ourselves in this
world. Our external narrative is the same
voice painting a picture of what this
world looks like.

I SEE A HUGE PROBLEM WITH THIS NARRATIVE.

When we only allow our internal
narrative to influence our worldview we
are missing the large pieces of
information.

Our brain will fill in information, because
we hate not having enough information.
Once we generate this information, even

though we don't know if it's true we call it "factual."

This happens for several reasons, our ego, the need for the brain to have reliable information, and because our brain hates not having the whole story.

This is why we have psychological biases. A good way to overcome psychological biases is to look for opposing information.

A second way to overcome these biases is to test them with action. This could lead to more information chasing, because our brains love more information. Just be careful to balance information with action.

Another problem arises because sometimes the power of storytelling is so great that we default to just listening to the internal narrative.

For example: You know you need to exercise, so you go to the closet to get your workout clothes and realize your workout shoes are in the car. Now your brain will process a myriad of reasons why you shouldn't go.

"You have to be at work in a few hours so you need to conserve your energy."

or

"Why don't we look up exercise on youtube that we can do in the living room so we don't have to go outside."

15 MINUTES LATER YOUR WATCHING CAT VIDEOS.

Your prefrontal cortex will churn ideas, possibilities, and alternatives while trying to think of other things. The mental mess can be chaotic at times.

You see your amygdala is like your drunk jerk uncle who always shows up to family gatherings, but he hates it. Your prefrontal cortex is like his wife that is always filtering what others say and do, so it doesn't upset your jerk uncle. You can't just kick your uncle out of family gatherings, well you possible could...but think about it like this:

You can't get rid of your amygdala, it's a part of the brain's family. Have you ever tried to just stop being angry? It doesn't work.

Have you ever tried to control your compulsive spending habits or your poor relationship choices?

Yes, but with no avail. It's because you can't kick the function of the amygdala out of your brain. All you can do is teach it not be as loud.

Resetting the problem solving loop is the same thing as making sure your family gatherings don't have alcohol.

That is why we must reset the problem solving loop. It's a great mental practice that allow us to clear away the mental clutter and keep that mental clutter out of our storytelling journey.

Focus, the flow state and taking action all come from optimum mental capacity, a benefit of resetting the problem solving loop.

In previous chapters we talked about exercises that help reset the problem solving loop. Here is a list of activities you can choose:

MEDITATION / MINDFULNESS

I use the headspace app to get clarity
sometimes before bed, sometimes first
thing in the morning. I would challenge
you to take a 30 day challenge to
implement a practice of mindfulness.
Amazon Eco has a free short version of a
meditation app called 1 Minute
Mindfulness. This is great if you don't
have time or if you feel you iffy about the
whole meditation thing. I assure you it's
a great practice that science shows will
make you happier and more focused.

JOURNALING

Journaling is a way that I stay grounded
and mindful in my daily tasks. I use the
bullet journal method to arrange my
tasks. Daily I will answer my question -
"What matters most?" and then I set
three intentions for my day. I also end
every task list with three things I am
grateful for. At the end of each week I

check my tasks to see my weekly
progress on my intentions.

WORK OUT

Physical Activity is a great way to get out
of the funk of a problem solving loop.
One physical activity that changes the
brain is a cold shower. Psychologist call
this hydrotherapy and it has been a
remedy for depression for a long time.
Van Gogh's doctors recommended ice
baths to help with his melancholy. The
science behind this is fascinating. Cold
showers help decrease stress hormones,
get our blood flowing from our skins
surface to the core, which move our
lymph, causing us to have more energy
as well as encourages our bodies to burn
fat. High intensity interval workouts or a
jump rope will do the same, so varying
your physical activity will help depending
on what kind of mood you are in.

Yoga, bike riding, a long walk in nature
or any other physical activity that causes
you to focus on breathing and movement
will reset the noise in the brain.

Step 4 - Finding A Mentor (We Learn How To Learn)

This is the most critical step because we still need information, encouragement, and feedback
in our Storytelling Journey. When we find a mentor, or coach, we have essentially traded poor feedback or proper feedback. The problem solving loop was fueling self doubt and sabotage. A mentor will equip you, encourage you, and give you the exercises needed to succeed.

A great mentor is going to provide you with a great "How." We understand what we need to do. If we have focused on our values we know our why. The how is where we get lost. A mentor should help develop a great how.

I highly suggest a mentor that is 10-20+ years older, who has worked in the field you want to pursue. I met my first mentor when I was in my early 20s. He wasn't looking for a student and I wasn't interested in learning from anyone. He needed help and I wanted to know how to become a better marketer and storyteller. Jaime lived in LA and I lived in San Antonio. I didn't have a steady job. Whenever Jaime needed a place to stay or a ride, in San Antonio, I would oblige him. I was able to get on commercial sets, I ran sound for a commercial and helped with a few national ad campaigns. I took what I learned and started a small business and did exactly what I saw my mentor do. By watching Jaime do work I was able to learn how to run a small marketing agency.

MENTORS CUT DOWN LEARNING TIME AND PROVIDE A ROCK SOLID ROUTINE / MAP TO MOVE YOU TOWARD YOUR HAPPILY EVER AFTER.

Mentors help you when you're stuck, fast-forward your learning curve and consult when you grow into a rock solid routine.

If you are completely unable to find a person in your field leverage the internet. Podcasts, audiobooks, learning courses and YouTube make it easier than ever to learn, gain experience, and cultivate relationships like never before.

ACT 2

Step 5 - Building Confidence (WE FIND WAYS TO WIN)

In story, a character always takes a step into the extraordinary. We don't have a Hogwarts, Shambala or Bat-cave to retreat into to study, train or achieve a zen state. When we talk about crossing the line into extra-ordinary we have to question societal norms. The largest opportunity we all have to improve on is in the area of confidence. Confidence is rooted in choice. American society has been largely developed in conjunction with the industrial revolution. Since the industrial revolution is over we need to re-evaluate our reasons for constructing society's pillars. Education, the market, government, housing development, and health care are built because of an old model of societal norms.

Baby boomers are confident in an old model of living and sometimes stick to comfortable ideologies that will not survive much longer. Generation X struggles because they have been brought up in a society that has changed dramatically from their childhood to now. Millennials are confident in technology, the connectedness of societies through technology, but struggle with fundamental societal norms like looking someone in the eye while communicating. Each generation is confident in different societal norms. This external narrative can build or detract confidence. Boomers may not be confident in hiring millennials; Millennials may not trust boomers as bosses.

We gain confidence by training. Confidence is taking action and accepting the outcome.

Confidence can help as much as hurt based on where we place our confidence. I am all for placing confidence in yourself, but I am also a proponent of placing confidence in feedback.

The easiest ways I have built confidence is:

DO WHAT YOU SAY.

The moment you say something and don't do it your confidence wanes. It becomes easier to lie to yourself and others about your goals and achievements. Research also shows when we talk about our goals to others we can be losing confidence. How? When we receive positive feedback about things we intend to do, our brain receives that feedback just as if we completed the task. That means talking about our goals gives our brains the dopamine hits, as if we completed the task. So, when we go to start the task, or when the task becomes hard we quit. Why work for the dopamine if we have already received it? Building in checkpoints with mentors helps. You will receive dopamine hits when you meet checkpoints, as well as when you meet with your mentor to talk about those checkpoints.

Share your work. Keeping a portfolio online helps for two reasons. You can attract clients with your work. You gain motivation and confidence as you see your body or work grow. Seeing growth builds confidence.

Box of why. I keep a shoebox filled with photos, quotes, mementos and scraps of paper that help remind me Why I do what I do. This helps me go back to my why. It's from the clarity of why that my confidence gets a boost to do what is needed. Otherwise, I would default to what feels good.

PHYSICAL ENDURANCE

Not only does working out help quiet the mind, strength training effects our confidence. When we realize our bodies are meant for endurance.

REPEAT THE SKILL

Our learning style always gets stronger when we practice repeatedly. Repetition matters when building confidence. I heard a quote that really stuck with me,

"Amateurs practice until they get it right, professionals practice until they can't get it wrong." Cultivating a habit of practice builds confidence.

Step 6 - Deeper Understanding (Know Yourself)

In the hero's journey, the hero finds allies, faces test, and finds he has enemies. This is a hard step to contextualize for many living in the western culture. While businessmen in the 1980s loved to read and espouse the writings of Sun Tzu, they didn't face the same realities of Sun. While movies provide great entertainment with seeing a hero character face life and death situations, the whole point of the test, allies and enemies is to develop the internal fortitude of the hero's values.

OUR GOAL IS HAVE A DEEPER UNDERSTANDING OF OUR OWN VALUES AND INTERNAL NARRATIVE SO WE CAN ADAPT AND CHANGE OUR INTERNAL NARRATIVE TO REFLECT OUR BEST SELF.

The best way I have found to do this is with psychological assessments. Business' use these tools in their HR departments to understand a myriad of personality types and how they will potential fit and work together. I have found that taking these test and finding core strengths, personality traits, and emotional tendencies help develop my self-awareness.

Once I have a deeper understanding of "who I am", changing the internal narrative to fit my strengths and weaknesses allows me to practice being the "manifesto me."

You can achieve the same effect of gaining personal insight by asking people around you a series of questions. I suggest the work that professional psychologist and business analysts have put into understanding self. I find the best allies in the storytelling journey are your personality strengths and traits.

Here is a list of personality tests / groups I recommend:

STRENGTHS FINDER 2.0

The reason I like Strengths Finder 2.0 is because it gives you five top personality values / strengths that you can leverage today to see results in your storytelling journey. While these strengths are based on values, which may seem arbitrary, your strengths are actionable. The book gives great suggestions on how to utilize these strengths in work, but they can easily transition to your personal life. This book is also a great team building tool.

ENNEAGRAM

The enneagram is an effective tool for understanding yourself in relation to those around you. It is based off of 9 personality types that shows our primary motivation in life. What I love about the enneagram is the ability to distinguish healthy personality traits vs destructive personality traits. Like in narrative work, enemies can become friends and friends can become enemies, so can personality traits give life or make it difficult. Enneagram is great for building teams, working through marriages or coaching others in life.

MYERS-BRIGGS

The Myers-Briggs test is a psychological test based on Jungian theories of psychology. Personalities are measured in 4 parts. First is the "Favorite World" do you enjoy the external world or internal? This is classified as Introversion or Extroversion. An easier way to understand Favorite World is how do you recharge? Do you need alone time or do you need to be around people? Second is "Information." How do you take in information? Do you use your sense to remember and process? Or do you find yourself using intuition, looking for patterns, analyzing data, and thinking before you make a move? Third is "Decisions." When making decisions do you like data, employing logic, and look to be fair? Does making decisions based on harmony, the good of others and what feels right make more sense in your decision making? Finally the last area is "Structure." You either take in the world around you by prospecting it or judging it. In work that may look like waiting too long to make a decision vs making a decision and missing new information. What is paramount is to understand that not one set of traits is better than the other. We are all going to have a different perspective on life based on our experiences. Myers-Briggs is an ally in the storytelling journey because it gives us multiple ways to process the world around us. This is a key strength because the more perspectives we have the better our skills become. How? The ability to look for common denominators in life allow us to communicate more effectively. As you will come to find out communicating your pain, your why, and your goals will be processed differently by people.

THE TABLE

The table is a group of guys I meet with monthly. We are all in a similar stage of life. We are all fathers, work closely in technology and have similar religious convictions. We are all progressive and have similar personality types. But what is most important is that we stay committed to trust and relationships. We discuss our failures, call each other out, and have cried together. Relationships matter and society has traded deep relationships for the convenience of shallow acquaintance. In the journey of life you need people who know you, ,who care for you and who will motivate you to life to the fullest.

Step 7 - The Approach to Extraordinary
(True Happiness Is Within)

Happiness increase not based upon circumstance, but upon our a set of factors. Studies show 50% of our temperament is set. 10% is set upon our financial situation. The other 40% is based entirely upon what we choose to do with our minds, time and body. That's good news! We have the opportunity to increase our happiness 40% with our actions and decisions.

In the storytelling journey, you need to understand your actions not only effect those around you, but your ability to be happy. Choosing the right things to occupy your time and your mind make happiness not a location or an event, but a very real process that can be lasting.

The center of your brain that produces dopamine produces less and less each year. That's why old people are so grumpy. Have you ever met a happy old person? You know what separates them from the others? Activity. They stay active. If you don't use the dopamine receptors in your brain, you will lose them. You need to be active starting today. Your happiness depends on it.

Ego is truly the enemy. We overcome the ego with focus. What does that mean? Getting into a flow state surpasses the ego. The ego is the judgmental portion of the brain that measures. Flow state is the state in which all 110 bits of information per second is being used in mental or physical activity. The flow activities should challenge us to work and think harder. This leaves no room for, pain, hunger, ego, or judgment. Setting a priority to do deep work, to focus and concentrate on flow producing activities increase the quality of our life and our work. I set the first part of my day to writing. I know that the first 4 hours of my day are the best hours I have to create deep meaningful work. When we guard our time and set the intention to work on flow producing activities, life gets better.

Scientifically speaking, more money doesn't mean more happiness. Why? We have a psychological bias called the "Hedonic Treadmill." This psychological treadmill tells us to consume our resources as they increase. Meaning, the more money you make, your mind finds a way to spend it, to grow into that new socio-economic class. The best way to overcome the hedonic treadmill is to set budgets and limits on spending. I have friends who set limits on their income. Not because they don't want more money, but because they know they can live a sustainable happy lifestyle and focus on the things that really matter. What happens if they make more money than expected? They usually live off of 50% of their income and place the rest in business, investments and charities. This mindset allows them to use money as a tool and not control their happiness.

Community plays another role in our ability to produces feelings of happiness. We are a connected species, when we choose isolation we limit the amount of happiness producing chemicals that our brains can manufacture. Sex is a huge part of being connected, but studies have shown that oxytocin is released during sexual activity. Oxytocin is meant to create lasting human bonds. When we introduce oxytocin into the body and it is not followed up with lasting relationships, we can suffer from depression. Happiness is found in community and loving relationships that last. Our culture's current "swipe right" hook-up on demand has very real emotional and psychological issues. The millennial generation is said to be the most stressed out generation. Comparatively high school and college students have as much psychological pain as a psychiatric patient in the 1950s. We have been eroding the line of community with shallow interactions. Lasting relationships are built on time, attention, being present, and sticking with a person through hard times.

Finally when it comes to happiness, we have to choose to operate from our intrinsic values. The values that drive the manifesto me, rather than the values others try to impose on your life. Japan is one of the most unhealthy countries on the planet. One reason is the unhealthy attitude towards work. Japanese business men live out of balance when it comes to work life. The culture places extrinsic values on wealth and the appearance of hard work. Japanese men don't think to question the values that society places in front of them. American youth do the same. We don't question the ideals of wealth, work, and how they relate to happiness. You have to choose yourself. You have to create your own values and live them.

There is a verse in the New Testament Bible about being able to distrust authority. John was a follower of the historical Jesus who appeared in the first century. Around the same time that

Christianity was gaining momentum as a religion, Gnosticism was making a resurgence by latching on to early Christian theology. What is amazing to me is that the early teachings of the gnostics looks exactly like America youth culture of today. The gnostics believed that nothing we do matters, there is a secret knowledge that allows us to be free and there is no set rules for society. John wanted to remind people, specifically followers of Jesus to remember their "Why" for themselves. He writes:

MY DEAR FRIENDS,
DON'T BELIEVE EVERYTHING YOU HEAR.
CAREFULLY WEIGH AND EXAMINE WHAT PEOPLE TELL YOU. MY DEAR CHILDREN, YOU COME FROM GOD AND BELONG TO GOD. YOU HAVE ALREADY WON A BIG VICTORY OVER THOSE FALSE TEACHERS, FOR THE SPIRIT IN YOU IS FAR STRONGER THAN ANYTHING IN THE WORLD.
THESE PEOPLE BELONG TO THE CHRIST-DENYING WORLD. THEY TALK THE WORLD'S LANGUAGE AND THE WORLD EATS IT UP.
(1 JOHN 4:1,4,6 MSG)

What amazes me is that the teachings of the Bible ask us to affirm our beliefs. To make our own choice and to believe we are created for a purpose.

There is one caveat to happiness. Angela Duckworth, author of the book "Grit" defines grit as, "perseverance and passion for long-term goals."

You will never be happy unless you commit long term to seeing your manifesto me come alive. You have to be willing to stay the course for your happily ever after.

Step 8 - Spending Yourself on Behalf of Others
(We Become A Solution)

The way that we share our pain mattes. I believe we should be not bottling our pain, but giving it expression, allowing it to fuel us. When we hide our pain, we are forgoing the shared human experience because shared pain creates empathy.

I find people get sharing pain totally wrong because they ask for empathy by leveraging their pain in order to manipulate or prove their entitlement to compassion and empathy. When we share our pain from a place of entitlement we damage the empathy experience because it is no longer shared. Sharing pain has to come from a place of humility and solution, if possible. There are some pains that are not "solvable." Sharing these pains becomes a shared language between those suffering in the same way.

How you process the pain is a solution in itself. Pain is the catalyst to great story. It is many times our inciting incident that leads us to change. There are other people out there struggling with your same pain points. The hero's journey is about discovering those pain points and trying to solve, cope, or change the narrative.

If you have journey this far in the storytelling heart, you begin to realize that the first 7 steps are a solution to bad narrative, the pain points you feel in life. Once you have implemented the storytelling process you should see change. This is where things get beautiful, when you share your story you activate others storytelling journeys. You build your character enough to be somebody else's solution.

When you start to use the storytelling tools for other people you can start a movement, a tribe or a community that resounds with your story and uses your story for their personal benefit. Ask somebody about their intrinsic values and if they are living up to them. Ask somebody, "what matters most?" Show someone the solutions for the getting out of the problem solving loop and on to a better life.

For me this step is about creating marketing material. You are the product and your story is your marketing. The problem you solved is your product and the steps listed above are yours to use in helping others. Why? Because you used the steps in your own context and have probably made discoveries of what works for you and what doesn't. The Storytelling Heart is not about following a step by step guide and then magically you become happy. It's about journey deep into self to find the fulfillment is tangible.

The other half of spending yourself on behalf of others is being brave. When you choose to be brave in the midst of pain, you have a tremendous advantage. Your audience, friends and loved ones are looking to you. Even when you don't think they are, they are. We are looking to you to make a positive impact around you. Your actions matter. Your actions reflect the emotional state you are in when you take them. Don't let your actions / decisions be based on fear, but take action and be brave.

ACT 3

Step 9 - Telling Your Story in a Compelling Way.
(How We Build Our Tribe)

"BUSINESS WAS ORIGINATED **TO PRODUCE HAPPINESS,** NOT PILE UP MILLIONS"
-B.C. FORBES

B.C. Forbes was the founder of Forbes magazine and a successful businessman. I find it very compelling that he chose to look at business as a happiness producing machine, not an investment, nor strategy for wealth.

Because we are storytelling animals, we pay massive attention to the stories around us. When we have a truly amazing story we have a truly transformative product. One massive mistake that took place in the 21st century was the idea that the medium is the message.
Marketing became noise, art lost it's subjective allure all because we made

things just because that should be enough.

I believe society is returning to understanding that deep meaning is a value that is transmitted by the medium. When we don't have a truly transformational product or service it doesn't matter how good your marketing is. Great marketing for a poor product spells doom for the longevity of that product.

Great products and services take time.

Why am I talking to you about business? Isn't this a book about story?

This is a book about story, but as you take a storytelling journey you become to awaken your innate talents and you start to see how valuable you are, and the value you add to others. When you add value to others that is business. We have the most opportunity to influence others by adding value to them in a free market.

Entrepreneurship is such a hot topic right now. Twenty years ago entrepreneurship was heavily frowned upon. Everyone thought unless you had big brand chain store, you were fraudulent or poor quality. With the explosion of the thought market brought about by the internet, we know quality and honesty belong in small business.

While you may not value commerce, your story has the ability to shape minds and markets if you are willing to help others. We live in a world where ideas, philosophies and mental practices are successfully sold in the market. If you are documenting your story journey on social media and find that you are attracting a crowd you should seriously think about being intentional about nurturing that relationship and taking it to the next level with a product, service or entertainment.

Your story is marketing, but many people don't tell their story in the most effective way. I not only encourage you to walk the hero's journey, but to share you story the same way.

Step 10 - Giving back
(How We Inspire Others)

I am a huge believer in practicing gratitude. Reciprocity is when our gratitude takes action. The quickest way to be happy is to share that happiness with someone else. We tell our story for many reasons, but a significant reasons is because we hold the answers to some of life's problems. When I find someone like myself who is struggling with the same problems I had I help them. I ask myself the question, "Where would I be now if I had access to a mentor, information or resources to activate my storytelling journey?

I love cinematography. I try and incorporate that into my life as much as possible. When friends are launching projects they come to me for marketing and promotional materials. Why? Because I am grateful. Gratitude is a relational currency. Relational currency is how we gain trust. When we give and expect nothing in return we gain something money can't buy. I encourage you to give you story, time, talent, or expertise to those in need. I'm not saying give it all away, but think about giving 10% to make the world a better place.

Step 11 - Burning Bridges
(How We Stay Focused)

I get angry when I see someone make such progress in life, in their journey and then throw it all away. It could be lack of self-discipline, poor relationships or manipulative leadership convinces them to throw it all away. In the hero's journey step 11 is The Resurrection or The Dark Night of The Soul. What I love about storytelling is that it keeps it real. Once you have seen massive changes in your life and you introduce those changes to those who are stuck, you will receive pushback. Our job is to not let others (or yourself) backpedal on the progress made. Life is a journey and we will all make mistakes, but throwing in the towel when we have journeyed this far is insane. There will be days when life doesn't go well. There will be days when you lose. When you answered the questions "What matters most?", you did so to define what your reality will look like. Sometimes you have to cut ties altogether with people, places and habits that hold you back. The idea of resurrection is that you can't go back because going back doesn't exist.

Burning bridges is a way to ensure that your story change will stick.

Step 12 - Transformed (How We Keep Going)

The hero's journey never truly ends. The hero's journey is about transforming yourself, in order to transform the world. If you take seriously the tools and resources in this book, you will be able to fight against the poor internal narrative and replace it with an internal narrative that fuels change, compassion and creation. This book is meant to be used by you to inspire others, to sell your ideas, to help others and to ultimately change the world around you for the better.

A GREAT STORY STARTS WITH YOURSELF. I HOPE YOU TELL THE WORLD A GREAT STORY.

ABOUT THE AUTHOR

Hey, My name is Nick Ovalle and I live in Riverside California with my wife and three kids. This book is the manifesto of my own personal growth. I follow these 12 steps in my personal life, professional life, marketing efforts, and cinematography. I hope that this book has inspired you to make a difference in your narrative. Drop me a line at nicholasovalle@gmail.com.

Proof

95649738R00113

Made in the USA
Columbia, SC
13 May 2018